Joyce
Marx
Hardy
Austen
Defoe Abbott Melville Montaigne Machiavelli Chesterton Cooper Emerson Hugo Grimm
Eliot
Stoker Carroll Christie Haggard Byron Molière
Wilde Maupassant Engels Schiller
Garnett Einstein Fitzgerald Hawthorne Smith Kafka
Goethe Dostoyevsky Hall
Cotton Kipling Doyle Willis
Baum Henry Nietzsche
Leslie Dumas Flaubert Turgenev Balzac
Stockton Vatsyayana Crane
Burroughs Verne
Curtis Tocqueville Gogol Vinci
Homer Widger Tolstoy Whitman Busch
Darwin Thoreau Twain Scott Plato Harte
Potter Freud Zola Lawrence Dickens Burton Hesse
Kant Jowett Stevenson Cervantes
Andersen Voltaire
London Descartes Burton
Poe Aristotle Wells Cooke
Hale James Hastings
Bunner Shakespeare Irving
Richter Chekhov Chambers Benedict Alcott
Doré Dante Swift Shaw Wodehouse Pushkin
Newton

Travels through the Empire of Morocco

John Buffa

Imprint

This book is part of TREDITION CLASSICS

Author: John Buffa
Cover design: Buchgut, Berlin – Germany

Publisher: tredition GmbH, Hamburg - Germany
ISBN: 978-3-8424-4512-3

www.tredition.com
www.tredition.de

TRAVELS

THROUGH THE

EMPIRE OF MOROCCO.

BY

JOHN BUFFA, M.D.

PHYSICIAN TO THE FORCES.

ILLUSTRATED WITH A MAP.

LONDON

1810.

PREFACE.

My motives for publishing this volume of Travels, will be best explained by a detail of the circumstances which gave rise to my journey to Morocco. In 1805, I was serving in the capacity of Physician to His Majesty's Forces, at the Depot Hospital in the Isle of Wight; whence, by dexterous management of the Army Medical Board[*], I was removed, and placed upon half-pay, in June of that year. At this period, it occurred to Mr. Turnbull, Chairman of the Committee of Merchants trading to the Levant, that it would be of advantage to the public, were the offices of Garrison Surgeon of Gibraltar, and Inspecting Medical Officer of the ships doing quarantine, which were then united in the person of Mr. Pym, separated and made distinct appointments; and he was pleased to think that, from my local knowledge, and other circumstances, I should be a proper person to fill the latter of these offices. This was also the opinion of His Royal Highness the Duke of Kent, Governor of the garrison. Representations were accordingly made on the subject, to the then Secretary of State for the War and Colonial Department, Lord Castlereagh; and it was so fully understood that the proposition had been assented to on his part, that an order was issued from the Transport Board, to provide a passage for myself and family to Gibraltar. There I waited some months, in the expectation that the commission would be sent after me, but in vain. In the mean time, I received a communication from Mr. Mattra, British Consul General at Tangiers, requesting that I would cross over to Barbary, and attend His Excellency the Governor of Larache, First Minister of the Emperor of Morocco, then labouring under a dangerous illness. It was on my return from this journey, that I found a letter from Mr. Turnbull (See Appendix, No. III. p. 227), stating that my old friends of the Medical Board had been at their usual work of persecution, and by their scandalous misrepresentations to the new Secretary of State for War and the Colonies, Mr. Windham, had succeeded in preventing the appointment which His Royal Highness the Governor of Gibraltar had been graciously pleased to design for me.

During my residence in Barbary it was my good fortune to gain the approbation and friendship of the Emperor of Morocco, and of the principal Officers of his Court, by which I was enabled to give facilities to the procuring of fresh provisions for our Navy, and render to my country other services, not strictly in the line of my profession. (See the various documents at the end of Appendix.) Having succeeded in restoring the Governor of Larache to health, and performed some other cures, acceptable to the Emperor of Morocco, I considered the objects for which I had crossed over to Barbary accomplished, and returned to Gibraltar, after having received the most flattering marks of distinction, both from the Imperial Court, and from Lord Collingwood, Commander of the British fleet in the Mediterranean. The letter of the Emperor of Morocco to His Majesty (Appendix, No. X. p. 239) is an ample proof of the disposition of that prince in my favour.

Finding the principal aim of my voyage to Gibraltar frustrated by the machinations of the Medical Junta, whom I have already stated as ever active in mischief, I determined to return to England. The letter of the Emperor of Morocco to His Majesty, and a general certificate, couched in the strongest terms of approbation, and signed by all the principal merchants of Gibraltar, I thought were documents, which, added to my correspondence with Lord Collingwood, and the officers of his fleet, would not fail to have procured me a favourable reception, and some attention to my claims.

But the letter of the Emperor of Morocco, as it still remains unanswered, I cannot but believe has never been presented to His Majesty. Nay, the pressing solicitations, with which I have since been honoured on the part of the Emperor of Morocco, through his principal Minister, to return to that country, I have hitherto been obliged to delay answering, that I might not, on the one hand, insult, by evasive or false replies, a government from which I had experienced such friendship and respect; or, on the other hand, be compelled, by a true statement, to compromise my own.

The principal design of publishing this account of my journey to the Barbary States, is to shew the good policy, on the part of this country, of keeping upon terms of strict amity with the government of Morocco. The neglect, which, on this occasion, has been evinced of the Emperor's letter, I cannot but consider, in a public point of view, as extremely reprehensible, independently of the private injury it has occasioned to myself. Whether this neglect arose from the misrepresentations of the Army Medical Board, or from those of any other persons, I will not pretend to determine; but in any case, a most censurable disregard, even of the forms of civility, towards a Prince, who, however we may affect to despise his influence in the great political scale, has it always in his power materially to promote or to impede the interests of this country in the Levant, must attach to some quarter or other.

[*] As the members of that body are expected shortly to be dismissed from their situations, I think it right, lest at any future period injustice should be done to innocent individuals, by confounding them with the guilty, here to state that Sir Lucas Pepys, Bart. Mr. Thomas Keate, and Mr. Francis Knight, Apothecaries, at present compose the body illegally calling themselves the Army Medical Board, whose conduct for a great many years has brought disgrace and disaster on that important department. For a detail of their conduct, see "An Analytical View of the Medical Department of the British Army, by Charles Maclean, M.D." 8vo. published by Stockdale, Pall Mall.

CONTENTS.

LETTER I.

Inducement for the Journey — Arrive at Tangiers — Its History — Situation — Inhabitants — Military — Governor — Fortifications — Subterraneous Passage — Socco, or Market — Adjacent Villas — Invited to
Larache.

No. II.—Letter from the Secretary of the Transport Board, informing Dr. Buffa that a Passage in one of His Majesty's Transports to Gibraltar was ordered for him and his Family.

No. III.—Extract of a Letter from John Turnbull, Esq. Chairman of the Committee of Merchants trading to the Levant, &c. to Dr. Buffa.

No. IV.—Extract of a Letter from John Ross, Esq. Acting Consul General at Tangiers, to Dr. Buffa.

No V.—Letter sent by a Courier from the Court of Morocco to J. Ross, Esq. by Permission of His Imperial Majesty's First Minister, after Dr. Buffa's having finally settled the Difference excited at that Time by the French Party in Barbary, between that Country and Great Britain.

No. VI.—Letter from Captain Stewart, of His Majesty's Ship Seahorse, to the Government of Morocco, for Supplies; which Dr. Buffa was directed to answer, after having procured the said Supplies without any Charge.

No. VII.—Letter from Admiral the Right Hon. Lord Collingwood, to the Government of Morocco, in answer to Dr. Buffa's Official Letter to Captain Stewart, touching on various public Matters.

No. VIII.—An Official Letter written by Dr. Buffa, by particular Direction of the Emperor of Morocco, in answer to a Letter of Lord Collingwood of the 8th July 1806, giving his Lordship Information of the happy Termination of the Negotiations which Dr. Buffa carried on, and which all the Representations of Mr. Ross to that Court were unable to effect; which gave rise to a very long and expensive Correspondence between Mr. Ross and Dr. Buffa, Long carried on by constant Couriers.

No. IX.—Letter written by Command of the Emperor of Morocco, to Lord

Collingwood, in favour of Dr. Buffa.

No. X.—Translation of a Letter from the Emperor of Morocco to the King. Referred to in the Petition.

Nos. XI. and XII.—Copies of two Letters received from the Government bf Morocco, to which Dr. Buffa has hitherto been unable to reply.

TRAVELS,

LETTER I.

Inducement for the Journey — Arrive at Tangiers — Its History — Situation — Inhabitants — Military — Governor — Fortifications — Subterraneous Passage — Socco, or Market — Adjacent Villas Invited to Larache.

Tangiers, January 12th, 1806.

I have long felt very desirous to visit a country, which, notwithstanding the many revolutions it has undergone, and the enlightened characters of its conquerors, is regarded as still immersed in a degree of barbarism almost unparalleled. It appeared to me next to impossible that a nation so contiguous to Europe, with which it has for centuries maintained a constant intercourse, could have remained in a state of such profound ignorance.

Impressed with these ideas, I readily embraced the offer of a friend to accompany him from Gibraltar to this place, intending to travel further up the country, should I meet with sufficient inducement from the result of my observations here. We landed on the first of this month, and the intermediate time I have employed in obtaining information relative to the town of Tangiers from the earliest tradition to the present time. As the particulars I have collected do not appear devoid of Interest, I flatter myself, you will be gratified that I should have made them the subject of a letter.

This town, which by the ancients was called *Tingis*, or Tingir, and appears to have been the metropolis of the *Western Mauritania*, or Tingitania, as it was named, to distinguish it from *Mauritania Cæsariensis*; according to Pliny and others, was first founded ed fay

Antæus (about a thousand years before Christ), the same who was afterwards conquered and slain by *Hercules*. The giant is supposed to have been buried here: and the report of Plutarch, that his tomb was opened by Sertorius, and a corpse sixty cubits or more in length, taken out of it, confirms the idea. But according to others, *Tingis*, or the present *Tangiers*, lays claim to a more ancient founder than *Antæus*. Procopius mentions, that in his time were standing two pillars of white stone, upon which were inscribed in the Phoenician characters the following words: *"We are the Canaanites who fed from Joshua, the son of Nun."*

A colony of Carthaginians settled here, and it is most probable that a flourishing trade was carried on by them, as the situation of Tangiers is extremely well adapted for that purpose. Indeed the name *Tingis*, in the language of the Phoenicians and Carthaginians, signifies an *emporium*. When the Mauritaniæ became subject to the Romans, in the reign of Julius Cæsar, Bocchus, the son-in-law of Jugurtha, having defeated Bogud, the king of *Mauritania Tingitania*, he became possessed of that country, and Augustus, or, as some say, Octavius, confirmed this acquisition to him; and the inhabitants of *Tingis* were allowed the privileges of Roman citizens.

I cannot discover any thing further remarkable of Tangiers from the time it became a Roman colony, and during the period it was possessed by the Saracens, till the latter end of the fourteenth century, when it was taken by the Portuguese, who erected fortifications and other public works. It continued in their possession for nearly two centuries; and was at length given to our King, Charles the Second, as part of the dowry of his consort Catharine, We did not keep it long; for, owing to the little harmony that subsisted between that Monarch and his Parliament, it was ceded to the Moors in 1684, after we had blown up all the fortifications, and utterly destroyed the harbour. Since that event, it seems to have been gradually dwindling into its present insignificance.

I have before observed, that the situation of Tangiers is well adapted to the purposes of commerce, being about two miles within the Straits of Gibraltar (or Hercules); but the ruins of the fortifications and harbour have rendered the anchorage in the bay of Tangiers very unsafe. This is a great obstacle to trade; very little is carried on there at present, and that little is by a few Jews, and lately, by a Spanish merchant of the name of Don Pedro.

The town being built on the declivity of that high tract of land called Cape Spartel (the Cape *Cottes* or *Ampelusian* of the ancients), it is seen at a great distance; but on entering the bay, it appears to the best advantage. It is defended by two martello towers, a castle, and a large battery; but I am confident that it could not withstand the attack of a few English frigates, and that such a force from the bay might destroy the town in the space of a few hours. Notwithstanding the vicissitudes to which this place has been exposed, it still possesses a superiority over the other towns in the empire of Morocco; it is the capital of the kingdom, and the residence of the Consuls General of the powers in amity with his Imperial Majesty. The houses of these foreign residents are constructed with great taste in the European style; the habitations of the Moors are neat; the air is pure and salubrious; the supply of excellent water, abundant; and the market cheap and plentiful. This combination of advantages renders Tangiers, in many points of view, an eligible residence. The European society, which consists almost solely of the families of the foreign consuls, is pleasant and agreable, The adjacent country is beautifully romantic; and the opposite coast and bay present a most delightful prospect. The Moorish inhabitants are all soldiers, very poor, and entirely subject to the arbitrary will of the Emperor. It is capable of furnishing, at a moment's warning, three thousand cavalry, and two thousand infantry and artillerymen; but these troops are badly trained, and without order or discipline: I attended their evening parade yesterday, and was truly diverted with the sorry appearance of their best militia-men, who were to mount guard for the night. These Moorish soldiers are remarkably addicted to cheating. It is probably owing to their excessive indolence, which prevents them from making the usual exertions for obtaining a livelihood, and induces them to adopt the more expeditious mode of extorting from strangers the means of subsistence; but as they are not often presented with an object of prey, they continually labour against the pressure of extreme poverty. Tangiers is under the government of Sidy Ash-Ash; who resides at Tetuan. He is by no means partial to the English, but devoted to France; influenced by French principles, and French interest. Excepting a few small armed vessels, fitted out for piracy, there is no shipping in the harbour. I have observed none for the purpose of commerce; all their goods are exported in foreign bottoms; and when they bring in a prize, the vessel remains unsold for a considerable length of time, and it is always disposed of to a foreign merchant.

Several remains of the European fortifications are yet visible; the Moors have repaired some, among which the western bastions still form a principal part of the strength of the place. The castle, which appears to have been built before the time of the Portuguese, stands in a commanding position upon one of the most prominent rocks of this coast. By an order of the Emperor, all the civil and military officers of this town are obliged to reside in it.

From this castle is a subterraneous passage containing many curious remnants of antiquity. On each side of the passage are ruinous apartments, which we may readily suppose to have been designed as places for the concealment of treasures, or receptacles for the dead. From the fragments of some urns I have collected, upon which are to be traced parts of inscriptions in the Punic character, I imagine this subterraneous place to have been built by the Carthaginians, for one or both of those purposes. It extends from the castle to several miles without the gates of the town; whence we may likewise infer, that it served as a means of escape in case of a sudden insurrection, or siege. Here are several superb mosques and commodious public baths.

The *Socco*, or market, is held twice a week (on Sunday and Wednesday), in a spacious sandy square, outside of the western gate, whereto the peasants bring all kinds of provisions, and other necessaries, which are sold at very low rates. Fish and every sort of wild fowl are brought in daily, and sold very cheap. Among the Consuls' villas, some of which are built near the spot where the *Socco* is held, that of the Swedish Consul is the most worthy of notice. The pleasure-ground is laid out with great taste in orange groves; the gardens abound in fruit-trees, and the Consul has made a curious botanical collection.

I have just been interrupted by Mr. Matra, our Consul. He called to request me to go up to Larache, to attend the Governor, who is

dangerously ill, and has sent here for an English physician. I intended to have continued a brief account of this empire, from the time
it became a Roman province to the introduction of Mahometanism;
also by what means the Moors became mixed with Arabs: but I
must reserve this for the next opportunity.

LETTER II.

Sketch of the History of Morocco — Road from Tangiers — Simplicity of the Peasants — Moors hospitable — Arrive at a Village — The ancient Zelis — Public Accommodations — Much infested with Vermin — Arzilla, a ruinous walled Town — Arrive at Larache.

Larache, January 1806.

Before I proceed to give you the particulars of my journey to this place, I shall fulfil tho promise I made you in my last.

The present empire of Morocco is properly the *Mauritania Tingitania* of the Romans, as the *Mauritania Cæsariensis* comprised Algiers, Tripoli, and Tunis; and was so called from the Emperor Claudius. *Tingitania* was not decidedly reduced to a Roman province till after the death of *Bocchus*. Augustus afterwards gave the two Mauritanias, and a part of *Getulia*, to the younger *Juba*, as a remuneration for the loss of his father's kingdom (*Numidia*). *Ptolemy*, his son, by *Cleopatra* (daughter of *Antony* and *Cleopatra*), succeeded him. In his reign, the Moors of this country were induced to revolt by a Numidian named *Tacfarinas*, who had served in the Roman army, and who, at the head of a set of barbarians accustomed to every species of robbery, assisted the revolt he had excited.

After a variety of successes and defeats, they were completely routed by *Dolabella*, the Roman General, and a body of Mauritanians sent to his assistance by *Ptolemy*, This conquest contributed to establish peace for a short time in these provinces; but at the death of *Ptolemy* (who was treacherously cut off by *Caius*), they again revolted, when *Claudius* first fixed a Roman army in *Mauritania*. His generals, though not without difficulty, succeeded in restoring tranquillity, which scarcely met with any interruption till the latter end of the fifth century, when the declining state of the Roman power favoured another revolt, in which the Moors entirely shook off the yoke of the Romans, assisted by the Vandals, under *Genseric*, who overran Africa, and obtained possession of most of the maritime towns. The Vandals were expelled in the seventh century by the Saracens, under the Caliphs of Bagdad, a ferocious and warlike race of Arabs, who, from conquest to conquest, had extended and removed their seat of government from Medina to the city of Damascus; thence to *Cufa*, and from the latter place to *Bagdad*; where they established their Caliphate authority.

Flushed with their success, and burning with the hopes of plunder, in the conquest of countries more fertile and richer, but less warlike than their own, they extended their arms as far as the western *Mauritania*. This country then remained for some time subject to the Caliphs of Bagdad, and was governed by their lieutenants, a set of cruel, arbitrary, and rapacious men.

The distance from the seat of government, and the oppressive manner in which the Caliphs ruled, excited universal commotion in this part, and considerably diminished their authority. Their generals, far from suppressing, openly encouraged these tumults, and severally aspired to the sovereignty. In the midst of these intestine broils, *Edris*, a descendant of Mahomet, fled into Mauritania, to avoid the persecutions of the Caliph *Abdallah*, who, to ensure the succession to his own family, had caused the kinsmen of *Edris* to be put to death. *Edris* first settled in a mountain, between Fez and Mequinez, called *Zaaron*, where he soon gained the confidence of the Moors. He preached the doctrine of Mahomet, and, by degrees, succeeded in establishing it throughout the country. These people, fond of novelty, and extremely susceptible of fanaticism, readily embraced a faith so well suited to their manners and inclinations. They elected him their chief, and invested him with supreme power; which he employed in reducing the Arab generals. From that time, the characters of the Moors and Arabs gradually blended, so that in after-ages, among the generality of them, scarcely any distinction can be traced.

As it is foreign to my present purpose to carry you farther into the ancient history of this country, I shall proceed to give you tho particulars of my journey to this town. I left Tangiers, escorted by a guard, consisting of a serjeant and six horsemen, accompanied by an interpreter, and my few servants. We rode for several hours, alternately through gardens and woods: the former full of fruit-trees; such as orange, lemon, fig, pomegranate, apple, pear, and cherry trees. The scene became every moment more interesting. As we advanced, the country assumed a variety almost indescribable. The contrast was every where infinitely striking. At one instant the eye was presented with fine corn-fields, meadows, and high hills; nay, mountains, cultivated to the very summits, are covered with immense flocks of sheep, and herds of cattle; while the vallies conveyed to the imagination an idea of the fertile plains of Arcadia; the simple manners of the Moors, who tend these flocks and herds, still further inducing one to believe them the happy, peaceful people, the poets feign the Arcadian swains to have been. On the other hand are huge mountains, bleak and barren, inaccessible to man, and scarcely affording food to the straggling wild goats that venture to browse on them.

There is a degree of simplicity in the behaviour of the peasants, so widely different from these who inhabit the towns, that it is impossible to suppose them the same race of men. From the great affinity between the manners and customs of these country Moors, and the *Scenite Arabs*, the inhabitants of *Arabia Deserta*, we may naturally infer that they must have derived those habits from the latter.

They reside in villages composed of tents to the number of forty or fifty, which they remove at pleasure; when the pasture fails in one valley, they strike their tents, and seek another, where they remain till the same necessity impels them to quit that in its turn. This was precisely the custom of the *Arabes Scenitæ*. The vast plains of sand with which *Arabia Deserta* abounds, were occasionally interspersed with fertile spots, which appeared like little islands. These we're rendered extremely delightful by fountains, rivulets, palm-trees, and most excellent fruit. The Arabs, with their flocks, encamped on some of them, and when they had consumed every thing there, they retired to others. Their descendants, the present *Bedoweens*, continue the practice to this day. The name given to this kind of village is the same as that of the Arabs just mentioned, which is *Dow-war, or Hbyma.*

The families of the Moorish peasants appear to be very numerous, as I observed that each tent was quite full. They flocked out as

I passed, to gratify their curiosity in seeing a *Massarane* (for so they denominate a Christian). Yet, notwithstanding their antipathy to all Christians, I was received with the greatest hospitality by these followers of Mahomet. They seemed to vie with each other in presenting the bowl of butter-milk, which they consider as a great delicacy, and. indeed, an offering of peace.

In the centre of a plain, about eight hours journey from Tangiers, we halted, and refreshed ourselves. After allowing my serjeant and guard to perform their ablutions, and say their prayers, we proceeded on our journey, and arrived, very late in the evening, at a village on the banks of a large river, which, from its situation, I imagine to be the *Zelis*, or *Zelia*, of the ancients, and which, by its annual inundation, fertilizes and enriches the country to such a degree, that, with very little labour, it produces abundant crops of all kinds of grain, particularly of wheat and barley.

A number of rivulets have their source in those mountains, which, joining others in their course, at length form pretty considerable rivers; and these, meeting with obstacles from the projecting rocks over which they pass, produce most beautiful natural cascades, which, precipitating themselves into the plains, preserve so great a moisture in the soil, that it is covered with a continual verdure.

There are no public inns for the accommodation of travellers on the road; but the Emperor has caused stone buildings to be erected, at certain distances, as substitutes. These buildings are not so good as many of the stables in England; they resemble the sheds, made, by farmers, to-give shelter to their cattle in tempestuous weather: yet, miserable as they were, I was glad to accept the offer of a night's lodging in one of them, not having provided myself with a tent.

The Cadi of the village conducted us to this delectable abode, which we found already occupied by six Moorish wanderers, who, in the Emperor's name, were ordered to turn out, and make room for me and my suite. Supper was brought me by the Cadi; it consisted, of boiled rice and milk, and some fresh-water fish, tolerably well dressed. When I had partaken of this homely repast, I prepared myself for rest, of which I stood in great need from the fatigues of the day; but, alas! my evil genius had determined otherwise; it seemed as if all the fleas and bugs in His Imperial Majesty's dominions had been collected, to prevent my closing my eyes; or it was, possibly, a legacy bequeathed, me by my predecessors. Be that as it may, I found them such very troublesome companions, that I preferred the night air to the prospect of being devoured before morning; I therefore wrapped myself up in a thick blanket, and slept, unmolested, in the open air, till after daybreak, when I found myself sufficiently refreshed to pursue my journey. Crossing the river, we passed through a ruinous walled town, called *Arzilla*, commanded by an Alcaid, under the Governor of Larache. This, which is a maritime town, lies at the mouth of the above river, and was, according to Strabo, Pliny, and others, a *Phoenician colony*; it was afterwards successively in the hands of the Romans, Vandals, Arabs, and occupied by *Aphonso*, King of Portugal, surnamed the *African*. It was abandoned by the Portuguese in 1471, when it fell under the power of the kings of Morocco.

I observed several ruins in this town and its vicinity, but could not stay to inspect them, It is inhabited by Moors and Jews, and is surrounded by gardens abounding with lemon, orange, and grape trees. On the evening of the same day we reached this place. I shall defer the account of my reception here, and the state in which I found the Governor, till my next.

LETTER III.

Conducted to the Governor — Medical Hint from his Secretary — Governor recovers — Larache — Its Harbour, Shipping, and Inhabitants.

Larache, February 1806.

On our arrival at this place, we were met, at the gates of the garrison, by the Governor's public Secretary, who conducted us to a house belonging to Mr. Matra, and afterwards accompanied me to the castle to visit my patient. On our way thither I requested the Secretary to give me his opinion concerning the present state of the Governor's health; I also asked how he had been accustomed to live, and how long he had been confined to his bed. "What do you mean," said he, "by asking such foolish questions? you are not a *tweeb*" (the name for a physician). I told him that I was. He continued: "That must be determined by your success or failure; if you succeed, you will for ever establish your fame in Barbary; you will be esteemed and respected by all the Moors; but, if you fail, and His Excellency should die under your hands, I would then advise you to make your escape as quickly and as privately as possible, and never to attempt to revisit this country." I confessed the weight of the encouragement and threats which he held out; and inquiring whether he meant to insinuate, that if the Governor died I should suffer death? and whether they always punished their tweebs thus when they dispatched any of their patients to the other world? he rejoined, "Not exactly; but consider, you are a Massarene, which makes a great difference." I then intimated that I would decline having any thing to do with his master, and would return to Gibraltar. "You do not think of such a thing!" he exclaimed; "it would be unworthy of your character and situation. But come; I will give you a few salutary hints, which may be of service to you; the rest you will discover at the bed-side, and on feeling the pulse of your patient, I wish you may succeed in recovering him; but I am afraid he is going, and that no tweeb on earth can save him."

He then informed me that His Excellency had been attended, for some days past, by a celebrated tweeb, who stood high in the public estimation; that he had pronounced the Governor's disease incurable, and he had, bled him so copiously, and so repeatedly, that "I verily believe," added the Secretary, "he has not a single drop of blood left in his veins; I would therefore advise you to administer some good cordials, and also some nourishment, to restore his lost vigour." By this time we had reached the castle. I found the Governor in a situation truly deplorable. He had been bled, as the Secretary described, *ad deliquium*, and reduced so low, that it was with great difficulty I could hear what he was desirous of explaining to me.

His body was covered all over with purple spots, and had every concomitant symptom of the blood approaching to a putrescent dissolution, I afforded him all the assistance in my power the same evening; and early the next morning, when I visited him, I found him somewhat easier; the next day better; and thus progressively mending; till yesterday he was sufficiently recovered to venture on horseback, and I trust he will, ultimately, be perfectly restored to health and spirits. He is about forty years of age, of a genteel appearance, exceedingly well informed, and reputed to be the most sensible officer in His Imperial Majesty's service, perfectly, *au fait* in the intrigues and politics of the Cabinet of St. Cloud, and other nations, He has always been, and is still, a very steady friend to the English,

During my stay here so many poor wretches applied for advice and medical assistance, that I have completely exhausted my stock of medicines, and I am, in consequence of this, obliged to decline the Emperor's invitation to his court. I shall return to Gibraltar for a supply, and shall then pay him a visit at Fez.

Larache is supposed to be the famous *Lixus*, or *Lixos*, of the ancients, and, consequently, was in great reputation in the earliest ages, Pliny asserts, that the giant *Antæus* occasionally resided here; and further adds, that Hercules vanquished him in this neighbourhood, as he supposes the gardens of the Hesperides to have been not far off. This I think very probable, as the Arabic name of this town is *El Arais*, signifying a place abounding in gardens; which is still the case. The vicinity of it is, indeed, rendered extremely delightful by the number of gardens. Pliny also makes the river Lixos (upon the banks of which the town stood), by its winding course, to resemble a serpent, or dragon, from which he intimates that this river gave rise to the fable of the Dragon guarding the golden apples of the *Hesperides*. Be that as it may, the situation of the present Larache gives great probability to the supposition of its being the reputed *Lixus* of the ancients. The learned Aldrete affirms the word *Lixos* be derived from לחישו, *Lachisu*, or נה־אלחישו, *Nahara Lachisu*, signifying *enchantment*, or the *enchanted river*. He observes, that the town of Lixos was situated near the banks of a river of the same name; and that the inhabitants of this country were supposed to possess uncommon skill in sorcery and magic.

Many wonderful things have been related of *Antæus*, by various authors, in his two residences of *Tingis* and *Lixos*. Pliny mentions a Roman colony having been settled here by *Claudius*; and I should judge this statement to be perfectly correct, from the number of Roman ruins observable in and near the town. It was in the possession of the Spaniards in 1610, but was retaken by the Moors before the commencement of the eighteenth century.

It is surrounded by good bastions and other works; some of which were constructed by the Spaniards, and the rest by the Moors. It is encompassed by deep trenches, with sluices to fill them with water from the river, The streets of this town are narrow and dirty, paved with large irregular stones, and consisting of abrupt ascents and descents, which render them unsafe to pass through on horseback.

Near the castle, at the extremity of the cape, facing the Atlantic, is an oblong square, surrounded by a piazza, supported by colonnades, where the shops of the merchants are situated, and where the market also is held. The cattle-market is kept in an extensive plain, to which you pass through a crooked way, out of the western gate. Thursday is the market-day.

Fresh water is extremely scarce, and the inhabitants are sometimes greatly distressed for want of it. Larache is a seat of government, and contains a spacious inland harbour; but the entrance is dangerous from the badness of its bar, which might, however, be removed with little trouble and expense, so as to render the harbour very commodious for shipping,

The harbour contains a portion of the Emperor's maritime force, which consists of four frigates, a brig, and a sloop of war, in very tolerable condition. This little fleet is commanded by an admiral, and sails every year in the month of May; when it cruizes about during the summer, picking up a few straggling vessels, and returns here to winter; in which time the sailors are twice a week exercised at the great guns. This town is now entirely occupied by soldiers and sailors, and their respective families. It did contain about two thousand Jews, whose business it was to purchase hides, wool, and wax, for several commercial houses established at Tetuan; but these poor people were obliged to leave this garrison, and take refuge in the neighbouring mountains, from a sudden and irrevocable decree of the Emperor, on account of their having sold some *aguardiente* to the sailors, which occasioned a great fight, that was attended with the loss of three Moors.

I have just received intelligence of the death of Mr. Matra; I am extremely sorry for this event, as, in him, we have lost a very powerful advocate at the court of Morocco: but it is no more than I expected, from the state in which I left him at Tangiers.

LETTER IV.

Excursion to Mamora, and thence to Salee — Friendly Reception by the Governor of the latter — Rabat — Tower of Hassen — Shella — Mansooria — Alcasser — Quiber — Its Socco, or Marketplace.

Larache, 1805.

To escape from the importunities of those poor creatures who continued to pester me for medicines with which I could not supply them, I availed myself of the convalescent state of the Governor, and obtained his permission to make a short excursion to the nearest seaport towns on the western coast. Escorted as before, I directed my way towards Mamora, a fortress about sixty miles off.

I halted frequently to observe the face of, the country, and could not forbear lamenting the little knowledge I possess in the art of drawing; indeed, I never had more reason to regret having neglected it than now, as it would have enabled me to present you with some very interesting views, to which my pen cannot do justice.

The beautiful intermixture of lakes, forests, and green vallies, forming most delightful landscapes, brought to my recollection those scenes I have so often contemplated, in my youthful days, on the borders of Switzerland. The lakes abound with all kinds of water-fowls, and fine eels; and are surrounded by villages, sanctuaries, and holy houses; the latter occupied by the descendants of the ancient *Maraboots*, who are held in the highest veneration by the Moors, and whose habitations are considered as sacred asylums, which are never violated, either by the civil or military power.

We ascended an eminence, upon which stands one of their most celebrated sanctuaries, built in the form of a pavilion, with four arched folding-doors, in the Gothic style, covered with varnished tiles of various colours, and embellished with curious Arabic characters. I was eagerly approaching, at the head of my little party, to gratify my curiosity, when a shower of stones, from the holy inhabitants of the neighbouring huts and tents, compelled me to desist; and after a retreat of one hundred yards, I sat down to refresh myself undisturbed.

From this hill, however, I had a better opportunity of surveying the beauties of the adjacent lands, which are very productive; and also to observe the windings of the river *Seboo*, which, taking its source in the neighbourhood of Fez, forms a junction with the river *Beth*, and falls into the Atlantic Ocean.

After journeying about a league, we crossed this river in a ferry-boat, and in a short time reached the fort of *Mamora*, which lies about two miles to the south of the river. This fort, after having been demolished by the Moors, was rebuilt by the Spaniards in 1604, and taken by Muley Ishmael in 1681. It is commanded by an Alcaid, and inhabited by about forty or fifty families, who gain a livelihood by fishing for shads and eels; with which they supply the adjoining country during the winter season.

We rested at this place, and feasted upon fried eels, which I found equal to those caught in the Thames. From *Mamora* we proceeded to *Salee* another maritime town, situated in the province of *Ben-hassen*, and at the mouth of the river *Salee*, which is formed by the junction of two small rivers. The Governor of that place being an intimate friend of my patient, I was most kindly and hospitably received by him; and elegantly entertained in one of his gardens, which are well laid out, and ornamented with several fountains playing into marble basins, as well as by several delightful streams of water.

Salee is a walled town, strongly defended by a large battery, mounting twenty-four pieces of heavy ordnance, and a redoubt which protects the mouth of the river. It contains about five hundred regular troops, three thousand militia-men, five hundred sailors, and a number of Moorish merchants and Jews. To the north of this garrison is a small town, in a ruinous state, inhabited by a few negro families. I was told it was built by Muley Ishmael for the accommodation of his favourite black troops. To the south, and on the opposite side of the river *Salee*, is the maritime city of *Rabat*, commanded by a black chief, and garrisoned with black soldiers.

It is defended by a fort and strong batteries, adequate to prevent a hostile landing. It contains several ruins of importance; among the most conspicuous of which are those of a large mosque, and the famous castle built by *Almansor* the *Invincible*, together with a superb square tower; which latter is still in a tolerable state of preservation, and is called the tower of *Hassen*. This tower is about two hundred feet in height, strongly built with cut stone, and most curiously decorated with Arabic characters. It contains a staircase of easy ascent to the top, whence I had a most extensive prospect of the Atlantic Ocean, where vessels are descried sailing at an immense distance.

The walls of Rabat are nearly two miles in circumference, and fortified by several square towers. Exclusive of its regular garrison, it contains four thousand militia-men, and about fifteen hundred sailors, besides several Moorish merchants and Jews; which latter live in a separate quarter.

This town, as well as Salee, is admirably calculated for trade, capable of furnishing foreign markets with large quantities of wool, leather, wax, and other important commodities. These contiguous cities are surrounded by gardens, watered by plentiful streams, which are artificially conveyed from a neighbouring spring, that takes its rise in a valley called *Tamura*, to the south of Rabat, and which also supplies all the houses of the two towns with fresh water.

Both places contain docks for building vessels, and several small corvettes in the Emperor's service winter in these harbours: but the roads, like those of Larache, are only to be frequented from the beginning of April to the end of September, on account of the shifting of the sand, which accumulates on the wind blowing from the south-west, when the bar is rendered unsafe for vessels to pass. Too great attention cannot be paid by commanders or masters of ships, on anchoring there, as a great number of anchors have been lately lost, and many vessels stranded.

Curiosity prompted me to inspect a small ruinous town to the east of *Rabat*, named *Shella*, supposed to have been built by the *Carthaginians*: but my approach was rudely prevented by the inhabitants; no Christian, nor even Jew, being suffered to enter, on account of its containing several tombs of their most celebrated saints, while in fact it is only a sacred asylum for malefactors, and all the rogues of the country.

To the south, and about eight leagues from *Rabat*, in a sandy and almost desert place, is a castle, in a most dilapidated state, called *Mensooria*, which was erected by _Jacob Al__mansor_, for the accommodation of travellers, and is still resorted to by the trading Moors and Jews, as a refuge at night from the attacks of robbers.

Conceiving it rather hazardous to penetrate further in useless researches, I returned to this place, greatly chagrined at having been foiled in my attempts to explore the remains of antiquities in *Shella*, and other places. I assure you, my disappointment was not owing to the want either of perseverance or resolution, but the serjeant of my guard was an ignorant bigot, and a great coward, therefore unwilling and unable to protect, or share any danger with me. On my return here, I dismissed him, and obtained another serjeant, and a new guard, from the Governor, who caused my dismissed serjeant to be seized; and ordered him the *pallo*; but, at my intercession, he was pardoned, upon his promising for the future to evince a more soldierlike conduct, when summoned on duty.

The town of *Alcasser-Quiber* being only three leagues from this place, I also went thither, to see the *Socco*, which is held once a week, and is frequented by a vast number of the inhabitants of the neighbouring mountains, who carry their produce, consisting of cattle, fowls, eggs, butter, soft cheese, and large quantities of wool, hides, and wax.

This city lies to the eastward of Larache, on the banks of the river *Luxos*, and is separated from the town of *Arzilla* by alternate vallies and plains, amongst which some remains of redoubts, apparently, for the protection and defence of camps, are to be seen, and near which that unfortunate battle was fought in 1578, wherein *Don Sebastian*, King of Portugal, lost both his army and his life.

Alcasser-Quiber is a place of some note, carrying on an extensive and profitable commerce with Tetuan and other places. The town and its environs suffer greatly by the occasional overflowing of the river Luxos, which might however easily be remedied; but the Moors have no notion of altering things; therefore, without endeavouring to secure themselves from a recurrence of such disasters, they allow their houses to be filled with water, and themselves to be, not unfrequently, washed out of them.

This town contains upwards of fifteen hundred families, exclusive of six hundred Jews, whose quarter is distinct from the Moors. It is commanded by an Alcaid, subject to the authority of the Governor of Larache, and ranks among the principal cities of the empire of Morocco.

LETTER V.

Leave Larache with an Escort — Curious Custom on returning from Mecca — Arrive at Tetuan.

Tetuan.

His Excellency the Governor of Larache being perfectly recovered, I took my departure from that city. For the sake of novelty, I proposed returning to Gibraltar, by this route, rather than by Tangiers. I obtained a letter of recommendation to *Sidy Ash-Ash*, and was accompanied by a strong guard, provided with a tent, and all other necessaries for the journey.

On my way hither, I was highly entertained by the Serjeant of the guard. This man had not long returned from Mecca and Upper Egypt. He spoke Italian tolerably well, was full of strange notions, and considered himself quite a superior genius. He told me, that he expected to be promoted in a very short time, and asked me, whether I were present at his public entry into the garrison of Larache, on his return from the sanctuary of Mecca. I smiled, and answered him in the affirmative. He asked me, why I smiled? "At the novelty of the exhibition," I replied, "in carrying you to all the mosques, and afterwards in escorting you in state to your humble habitation." — "It is but too often the practice," rejoined he, "of petulant infidels to ridicule us, in the exercise of pious customs and religious duties." Then spurring his horse, he muttered something abusive, which I pretended not to hear. However, I found no great difficulty in appeasing the pious and sanctified serjeant. In short, I dispelled all his glooms and ill humours, and drowned his scruples, in a cup of port wine. It is customary among the Moors, when any of them return from the pilgrimage of Mecca, to go out in great procession to meet the devout pilgrim, whom some of them carry on their shoulders with great solemnity through the town and to his own house, where he sits in state for three days, receiving visits and donations from all classes of people, who flock with the greatest eagerness to obtain a sight of him. The conversation was insensibly renewed, and he told me, that of a company of fifteen pilgrims, who set out for the holy city of Mecca, he was the sole survivor, the others having all perished in the deserts. He was the only favoured and true believer that was permitted to visit the holy sepulchre. He added: "As the dangers attending the pilgrimage are great and various, does not the happy being, who returns safe to his native place, deserve the honours and compliments paid him, for his great perseverance and patience in such a dangerous undertaking, the success of which is the result of his innate rectitude?" I gave him to understand that he had made the case clear. "The French," he continued, "had a design upon the treasures of Mecca." I agreed that they certainly had; and asked him, by what power he thought the French army was prevented from possessing itself of Mecca. "Unquestionably," rejoined he, "by the invincible and invisible power of our Prophet." In reply to my intimation that it was the British arms which defeated the French before Acre and Alexandria, and compelled them to give up the conquest they had made in Egypt, he went on to say, that "all the great acts of mankind are guided and governed by a supernatural power. The French were defeated by the English, because the latter fought under the invincible standard of *Mahomet*; and so fully convinced are the true believers of this, that we now consider the English as brethren. I hate the French mortally; they are a set of bloody impious infidels, and treacherous to a degree; I would not escort a dog of a Frenchman for all the treasures of the Emperor; I would rather lose my head than protect one. I fought the dogs in Egypt; but I took care not to spare one; I laid many of them in the dust. It behoves every honest Moor to be on his guard against the intrigues and duplicity of the French. A Moor can certainly face six of them. The Emperor's troops have more bodily strength than theirs. By the by, it is whispered about, that they intend paying us a visit to plunder us, and ravish our fine women. Let them come, we will meet them, I warrant you, and give them their due. Not one will return to France to tell his story." I then filled him another cup of port, to drink destruction to the French, whenever they should attempt either his shores or ours—and here ended our dialogue. I found him a *bon-vivant*, willing to overlook certain restrictions of his Prophet, and to drink his wine like an honest Englishman.

The second day of our journey I had raised his spirits to such a height, that he wantonly picked a quarrel with the muleteer, and gave him two or three slight cuts with his sabre, which so much provoked the honest driver, that, being a stout robust man, he soon dismounted my hero, and would actually have sent him to the shades below, but for my interference. When the Serjeant recovered his senses, he was very much alarmed lest his conduct should be exposed, or reach the ears of the Governor of Larache. In order therefore to dissipate the fears of this gallant soldier, I made the muleteer and the other swear, by their Prophet, to keep the transaction a secret. After this we travelled on merrily, without further disputes, and arrived here on the third day. I waited immediately upon, and delivered my letter to the Governor, who commanded one of his officers to conduct me to the house of the Vice-consul, where I now remain, in expectation of some vessel to convey me to Gibraltar.

LETTER VI.

Ill Usage of a Lieutenant of the Swiftsure — Disaffection of the Moorish Governor towards Great Britain.

Gibraltar, March 1806

His Majesty's ship the Swiftsure having arrived at Tetuan, to take in fresh water, I went on board. The watering-place is about eighteen miles from Tetuan, and six from the customhouse, at which last place is a tower, guarded by a strong detachment, and commanded by a Captain. When the ship had completed her water, signals were made to strike the tent, and every one to repair on board.

It has always been customary for English men of war going to water there, to make the commanding officer a present of a cartridge of powder, which compliment was duly paid by the second Lieutenant of the Swiftsure; but the Moorish Captain, not contented with one cartridge, insisted upon having two. The Lieutenant refused to comply with this new and extraordinary demand; upon which he was immediately seized by a party of soldiers, who, after knocking him down, pinioned him, and in this degrading manner marched him up to Tetuan, under a strong escort.

Captain Rutherford (who commands the Swiftsure), on hearing of this daring outrage, could with difficulty refrain from making instant reprisals: but unwilling to embroil the two nations, he sailed without delay, and arrived in the course of a few hours in this bay. Two days after Mr. Wickes, the Lieutenant, joined the Swiftsure. He reports, that, after a most painful march, he was taken before Governor Ash-Ash, who released him, immediately, and promised to punish the Captain of the fort for the insult; a promise which, I am pretty confident, he never performed.

Such an act will naturally inspire you with horror, and induce you to consider the Moors as a ferocious, barbarous set of people: but, believe me, it could only have been perpetrated under the government of *Ash-Ash*. At any other port of Barbary, a British officer will meet with a most kind and hospitable reception, and every mark of respect due to him. The Emperor has given Ash-Ash positive orders to respect the English, and not to take the part of the French, directly or indirectly; but, as I observed in a former letter, I conceive this Moor to be completely under French influence.

I am extremely busy in making the necessary preparations for my next trip; and as you are kind enough to say you are gratified with the account I have already sent you of the empire of Morocco, and wish me to continue my remarks, I shall most probably trouble you with a letter, whenever I meet with any thing that may serve to interest or amuse you.

LETTER VII.

Sail for Tetuan — Appearance of the Coast — Enter the Boosega River — Curious Towers of Defence — Custom-house-Female Dress — Enter Tetuan over a Road of unlevelled Rock — Disagreeable Streets — Well received by the Governor — Public Markets — Socco — An Auction Market.

Tetuan; March 14th, 1806

One of His Majesty's brigs having been appointed to convey me either to Tangiers or Tetuan, the wind blowing due west, we sailed for this port. As the ship drew near the shore, I had a full view of this wild coast. The tops of the lofty mountains are prodigious barren rocks, while their base is interspersed with broom and box. The hills and dales are covered with myrtles of various kinds, assuming different shades of lovely green. The towers and castles, which are of a delicate whiteness, rising in the midst of these groves of myrtles, render the scene interesting. The plaster made use of in the erection of these towers is, of itself, extremely white; but the Moors are not satisfied with this, and they add a whitewash of lime.

The towers are harmless as fortifications, since, for want of skill in the manufacture of gunpowder, the Moors are very deficient in that necessary article. No present therefore is more acceptable to them than a few cartridges of it.

After firing two or three guns by way of signal to the Vice-consul, announcing my arrival, as the Captain had directions only to put me on shore, and to proceed to sea immediately to join Lord Collingwood's fleet, my baggage was put into a large Moorish boat, and I entered the river *Boosega* (commonly called St. Martin) in the Captain's barge. This river is defended by a castle of singular construction, the entrance to which is by means of a ladder to a door in the upper story, and which ladder is occasionally drawn up. The four angles of the building are finished with small turrets, capped with clumsy domes, and having several ports for cannon. Near this place many of the Emperor's gallies anchor, and winter.

Having proceeded a considerable way up the river, we landed at another castle, called the Custom-house. On my landing, I was received by the Vice-consul (an opulent Jew, and a native of Barbary), accompanied by the commanding officer and his troop. They conducted me to the Custom-house, which is built of stone, and whitewashed, arid, at a distance, appears to very great advantage. We entered this public building by an arched gateway, and proceeded through a winding passage into a quadrangle, in the centre of which is a well of excellent water. Near the well was an arcade, shaded by a grape-vine, to which I was conducted, and there placed in an old arm-chair. The Vice-consul and the Moorish commandant seated themselves cross-legged, upon mats spread upon the floor, and dinner, consisting of roasted fowls and fried sardinias, was immediately served.

After dinner my baggage was put upon mules, and a saddle-horse was brought for me. This animal was perfectly white, and loaded with an enormous saddle, which had a large peak before and behind, covered with a scarlet cloth, and furnished with a pair of stirrups of a curious form, much resembling a coal-scuttle; but, *outré* as this appeared, I assure you, I found myself very comfortably seated, and perfectly secure from falling. Thus equipped, we set forward for Tetuan, accompanied by a Moorish officer and twelve horsemen.

Whips are not in fashion in this country, and their place is supplied by two long ends of the bridle, cut to a point; but the horses, though very spirited, are perfectly under command, and need neither whip nor spur.

The town of Tetuan is seen at a great distance, from being built, like Tangiers, on the declivity of a high hill, and the houses being whitewashed. The road from the Custom-house is abominably bad; it lies across a wearisome, barren plain, surrounded by craggy mountains. Here and there, indeed, may be seen a small fertile spot, covered with cattle, sheep, and goats, and occasionally a well, encompassed by a wall of broad flat stones, capable of affording a seat to a dozen people. On approaching the city, however, the country appears more cultivated, luxuriant, and rich.

The figures of some common women, apparently employed in agricultural occupations, struck me with surprise, as their dress was quite different from any I had seen when in this country before. On their head they wore a straw hat, of an enormous circumference;

under this was a piece of white cloth extending over the forehead to the eyes; and immediately below this another, which reached as far down as the chin; their eyes peeping through the intermediate space. Their bodies were enveloped in a coarse haik, a species of serge of their own manufacture.

Upon entering the city gate, one of my guards took hold of my bridle, and conducted me over innumerable rocks, to the Jewish town. The surface of the ground being an uneven rock, which every where remains unlevelled, the streets consist of abrupt ascents and descents, even worse than those of Larache; they are also extremely narrow and dirty; and as the houses have no windows towards the streets, you in fact pass along between two dead walls, almost suffocated by a hot and fetid atmosphere.

When we reached the house of the Vice-consul, I was presented with a glass of *aguardiente*, for refreshment. After having passed the evening in the company of a numerous party of Barbary Jews, I retired to bed; and in the morning I waited on the Governor, to pay my respects to him. On our way thither, I was not a little surprised to see our Vice-consul pull off his slippers as we passed the mosques, and walk bare-footed. I soon learned, that the Jews are compelled to pay this tribute of respect, from which Christians are exempt, although they do not escape very frequent insults when walking through the city.

We found His Excellency sitting cross-legged on a tiger-skin, smoking his pipe, under a niche in one of the courts of his mansion. He received me with great politeness, and assured me that every thing should be arranged to render my journey to Larache safe and agreeable. Both, the Governor and his secretary asked me numberless questions respecting the laws and manners of the English; to all of which I gave short and general answers.

As we returned from the castle we passed through a street of unusual breadth, on each side of which were the shops of the merchants. I thence proceeded to take a general survey of the city; examining the different places allotted to people engaged in various branches of trade, and the manufactories of silk, carpets, and mats; and afterwards went to the public markets for meat, poultry, vegetables, cattle, sheep, horses, and mules. They are in spacious squares, and are exceedingly well stocked. I next went to see the *Socco*, which is a place appointed for the sale of several articles of wearing apparel as well as all sorts of goods, by public auction. The auctioneer walks backwards and forwards, exhibiting the commodities for sale, and bawling out the different prices offered. We returned, through several intricate streets, to the Jews' quarters, much fatigued, and worried with the impertinence and curiosity of the inhabitants.

LETTER VIII.

Tetuan — The Jews much oppressed there — particularly the Females — Costume — Singularity of the Streets in the Jewish Town — Ceuta — Would be invaluable to England — Melilla — Summoned to visit the Emperor.

Tetuan, — — 1806.

There is little that is remarkable in this town, beside what I mentioned in my last. It is distant twenty miles from *Ceuta*, a Spanish fortress, and twelve from the Mediterranean, and is nearly opposite to the rock of Gibraltar. It has a good trade, and contains about eighty thousand inhabitants, twenty thousand of which are Jews, said to be very rich. The Jews are tolerably civilized in their manners, but are dreadfully oppressed by the Moors. Seldom a day passes but some gross outrage or violence is offered to the Jewish women, the generality of whom are very handsome, though their dress is by no means calculated to set off, but rather to detract from, their beauty.

Men, women, and children, still preserve the same costume as in the time of Moses. You cannot conceive any thing more ridiculous than the *tout ensemble* of a Barbary Jewess in full dress. Every part of her apparel is rich, but is so heavy, that, to an European, nothing can appear more awkward and unbecoming. The Jewish ladies wear immense ear-rings. I have observed several full twelve inches in circumference, and of a proportionate thickness; and a few ornaments being affixed to the ear-ring, I leave you to judge what materials their ears must be made of, to bear such a weighty appendage.

The Jewish town is quite distinct from that of the Moors; but the difference between them is very little: the streets are equally narrow and dirty, and the houses have no windows on the outside; the roofs are also quite flat; the only variation is, that the streets are covered with a roof extending from the houses on each side, and have the appearance of subterraneous passages. There is a regular communication between the houses at the top, which is the favourite scene of recreation. Some of the women scarcely ever take the air, excepting on these flat roofs: in short, the inhabitants, both Jews and Moors, dance, sing, and take all their amusements on them. The rooms of the Jewish houses (as well as of the Moors) are long, narrow, and lofty, resembling galleries. Most of the houses are occupied by several families, which are generally large. Those inhabited by the more opulent are kept tolerably neat, and are adorned with rich and curious furniture; but they are, for the most part, exceedingly dirty; and the exhalations from the garlic and oil, which they use in great quantities in frying their fish, are enough to suffocate a person not entirely divested of the sense of smelling. Their taste is so exquisitely refined, in regard to the oil they use, that they prefer our lamp-oil to any other, on account of its high flavour.

Notwithstanding all these apparent obstacles to health, they contrive to preserve it admirably well. To an Englishman, their mode of life would scarcely appear worthy to be called living, but merely vegetating. Since the last plague, however, in Barbary, which destroyed a vast number of the Jews, they have not suffered from any infectious or contagious disorder, and their population has augmented so prodigiously, that the Emperor must, however reluctantly, extend the limits of their town. The Jews marry extremely young. It is not at all unusual to see a married couple, whose united ages do not exceed twenty-two or twenty-three years.

I cannot quit Tetuan, without giving you some account of *Ceuta*, which is at so small a distance from it. From its situation, it perfectly corresponds with the *Exillissa* of *Ptolemy*, being the first maritime town to the eastward of the ancient *Tingis*, or modern Tangiers. It also clearly appears to have been the *Septa* described by *Procopius*, who, with many others, derives this name from the adjacent seven hills. It was a place of great note in the time of the Vandals. It is now a strong regular fortified town. Ceuta is thirty miles from Tangiers, and nearly opposite to the entrance of the bay of Gibraltar. It is nominally still in the hands of the Spaniards; but it is confidently rumoured, and believed, to have been ceded by treaty to the French.

This important fortress has been, and is still, occasionally most awfully distressed for want of provisions; insomuch, that if closely besieged by land, by the Moors, and blocked up by the English by sea, it could not hold out any considerable time in possession of the French. The advantages resulting to Great Britain from such a valuable acquisition are incalculable.

Every person who is acquainted with the situation of Ceuta, the rival of Gibraltar, must be very much astonished, that it should still be permitted to remain in the possession of the Spaniards, since a squadron of men of war, and a flotilla of gun and bomb vessels, might reduce it, even without the assistance, of the Moors; and thereby England would be sole mistress of the entrance to the Mediterranean. Convoys could collect in safety at Ceuta, and our trade in this sea be comparatively secure from annoyance. I understand this place was closely invested by Muley Yezid (the late Emperor of Morocco, and brother to the present Emperor), but for want of proper co-operation by sea, where it is most vulnerable, he was necessitated to raise the siege, and withdraw his troops.

This garrison is supplied with provisions from Spain, the Moors being prohibited, on pain of death, from sending their commodities thither; and in order that this interdiction may be strictly observed, picquets and posts of Moorish cavalry and infantry are so judiciously stationed, that it is impossible for the mountaineers to smuggle in the smallest article. The supplies from Spain are extremely precarious, from the necessity of conveying them in small fishing craft, to prevent their falling into the hands of the English.

Melilla also is in the possession of the Spaniards: this maritime town lies to the eastward of Tetuan. Many authors assert it to have been founded by the *Carthaginians*. It is likewise called *Melela*, from the great quantity of honey annually obtained in its neighbourhood. It was taken by the Spaniards about the beginning of the fifteenth century, and has remained under their dominion ever since. It has a strong castle, built on a rock, named *Gomera*. Along this coast, particularly from Tetuan to Melilla, there are several coves, in which the Spanish gunboats, and other small armed vessels, find shelter in cases of necessity. Indeed *Melilla* is itself a place of refuge for those vessels of the enemy fitted out for the annoyance of our Mediterranean trade.

I shall conclude this with a copy of a letter, which I have just received from Mr. Ross, the acting Consul-general in the room of the late Mr. Matra:

"DEAR SIR, *Tangiers,*

"I heard only to-day of your arrival at Tetuan, on your way to Larache; and this evening I received a letter from Sidy Mahommed Eslawee, Governor of that place, to request, that, if I knew you were in this country, I would beg you to use, every possible endeavour to come to him at Larache, and to accompany him to the Emperor, who wishes very much to see you. Let me therefore request your repairing as quickly as possible to Larache, and joining him before he departs; but should you miss him, he has left orders with his Lieutenant-governor there, to forward you on immediately. I should hope this jaunt will prove highly beneficial to you. Nothing on my part shall be wanting, either in advice, or information, by which you may think I can be of service. If you should see Governor Eslawee before my letter reaches him, give him my kindest and best wishes; and say that I hope, as he has been for a great many years past a sincere friend to the British nation, his friendship will continue true and steadfast.

"I remain, dear Sir,

"Your most obedient humble servant,

(Signed) "JOHN ROSS,

"To Dr. Buffa,

Tetuan."

In consequence of this request, I am making preparations for my departure by to-morrow morning. I shall write to you again from Larache. Though I have described every thing worthy of notice in

that town in a former letter, yet I know you will wish to learn how I
am received by the Governor on this my second trip.

LETTER IX.

Journey to Larache — Annual Socco of St. Martin — No Christian permitted to witness it — Express Order for that Purpose in the Author's Favour — Specimen of native medical Skill — Reception at Larache — Complain of the Impositions of Governor Ash-Ash — Comparative Tariff — Effect the Renewal of the old Tariff with increasing Advantages.

Larache.

Before I introduce you a second time to the Governor, or relate my reception from him, I must beg leave to give you a description of my journey hither. Methinks I hear you say, "That is unnecessary, as, no doubt, it was much the same as before." No such thing, I assure you; for, in the first place, my style of travelling was infinitely superior, being provided, by the Moorish Governor, with a double guard, and having also eleven mules allowed me to carry my baggage, which, with two muleteers, my interpreter, and servant, made no despicable appearance. I had, besides, to contend with very stormy weather, which gave the country quite a different aspect. From incessant rains, the rivers had overflowed, and nearly the whole of the country was under water, which rendered our journey not only difficult but dangerous. We were obliged to halt for two days, near a village, till the waters subsided; and during this time we feasted on fine fresh-water fish, and wild fowl. On the third day we proceeded; and here I must not omit an occurrence which served still further to give me an insight into the general character of this once powerful people.

Fortunately (or unfortunately, some would say, who weighed the perils I had to encounter in the accomplishment of my wishes) I passed, on the day the inhabitants were meeting, the annual Socco of St. Martin, so called from its being held at the place whence the river of that name takes its source. I did not pass immediately over the spot, but so near, that I could perceive a multitude of people assembled together. To obtain a better view of what they were about, notwithstanding the representations of my conductors, that no Christian was suffered to be present at this fair, I proceeded towards the crowd; but before I could reach the place, I was assailed by hundreds of people, who saluted me with such a discharge of stones, and even some fire-arms, that I was extremely glad to make good my retreat, which, with the aid of my guard, I effected, without sustaining any injury.

Enraged at being thus foiled in my attempt, I hit upon a plan the most likely to succeed in gratifying my curiosity; which was, to send the Serjeant to the Cadi, to insist upon going up to the fair, and threatening to complain to the Emperor if he refused me. This had the desired effect. A deputation was ordered by the Cadi, with assurances that I was welcome among them. Accordingly, I repaired once more, to the scene of action.

The great show of cattle, sheep, &c. exposed for public sale, by men and women half naked, first attracted my attention; which was however soon diverted from them to a Moorish juggler, and a rope-dancer, the latter performing several feats of great muscular strength. The people had formed a complete circle, sitting cross-legged round the rope-dancer. He was making a good collection, when the arrival of a celebrated *tweeb* (the native term for a physician) spoiled his sport. At the sound of an instrument somewhat resembling a horn, they all started up, and flocked to the standard of this professor of the healing art, leaving the poor rope-dancer to finish his performance, or not, as he pleased. I found this new constellation to be a doctor of high renown, and a reputed saint, who lived in a neighbouring village, and who, as was his custom, had condescended to honour this annual meeting with his presence; selling and dispensing his medicines, arid at the same time performing surgical and dental operations.

In order to have a full view of this Moorish Esculapius, I approached as closely as the multitude collected round him would allow. He was attended by a negro slave, and two disciples. Ere long, four Moors brought a poor emaciated wretch, to obtain advice and relief from this redoubtable doctor. The unfortunate man was unable, from his reduced state, to stand. Having examined the eyes, tongue, and face of his patient, he made a solemn pause, and appeared to deliberate very profoundly, at length, he decided upon bloodletting *ad deliquium,* and immediately took from his patient eighteen ounces of blood; nor would he, in all probability, have stopped there, had the strength of the poor man allowed him to continue; but having brought on a *syncope,* he was obliged to desist. The arm was tied up with a handkerchief; the doctor received his fee from one of his patient's relatives; and the patient was left entirely to the efforts of nature in his favour. For humanity's sake, I afforded him every assistance in my power, and, after much difficulty, succeeded in restoring him to his senses; but he was so weakened by the absurd treatment he had experienced, as to have no chance of surviving the day. As the multitude firmly believed him to be quite dead, this apparent resuscitation astonished the people beyond measure; and from this circumstance supplies of every kind of provision were poured in on me, from all quarters.

Soon after the above scene, a young woman presented herself, afflicted with a violent tooth-ache. The doctor, after his usual deliberation, resolved to extract the dolent tooth; and taking a string from his box, he fastened it round the tooth, and by a sudden jerk (which, from its force, I expected would have brought away jaw and all), he drew it out. The poor girl bore the operation with exemplary patience and fortitude; and having satisfied the sapient doctor, she retired.

Whilst I was thus occupied in observing the wonderful proceedings of this singular practitioner, an uproar in another part of the fair attracted my notice. Curiosity prompted me to inquire into its cause, and I found it was occasioned by a wild mountaineer, who had been detected in the act of stealing a Moorish garment. He was seized, and taken before the Cadi, who ordered him the bastinado immediately; which was inflicted with such severity, that I could not forbear interceding for the fellow. The Cadi kindly remitted part of the punishment, and the culprit was set at liberty.

Finding nothing else likely to compensate my longer stay, I summoned my suite, and proceeded on my journey, reflecting on the mutability of all earthly prosperity, which was so strongly exemplified in the history of the Moorish nation. The scene I had just left, argued such a small remove from absolute barbarism, that, more than once, I could not avoid exclaiming: "Are these the descendants of those people, who, for so many centuries, gave laws to the greater part of Spain, and subjected whole provinces to their dominion? But those times are past, and, 'like the baseless fabric of a vision,' left 'not a wreck behind'."

After a journey of six days (which might have been performed in three, but for the delays I have spoken of), we arrived here. His Excellency the Governor, and his suite, came out to meet me. He embraced me very cordially, and conducted me to the castle, where I was served with a sumptuous collation. The Governor being in hourly expectation of the orders of his Sovereign to repair to court, has his route made out, and has requested me to keep myself in readiness to depart at an hour's notice.

I have received several letters by express, from, our Consul-general, complaining of Governor *Ash-Ash*, who has refused granting the regular supplies to our fleet, and the garrison of Gibraltar. From the character I have given you of this man, in a former letter, you will feel less astonished, when I inform you of his shameful conduct. His rapacity and avarice are unbounded. He refuses the regular supplies, insisting upon an additional duty being paid, besides the enormous one already imposed, on articles furnished to the English, contrary to the tariff established by treaty. Accordingly, I laid the following copy of the original tariff before His Excellency, and subjoined the imposition of Ash-Ash. *Order to be observed by the British Vice-consuls, at Tetuan and Tangiers, respecting the English.*

DUTY.
Spanish Dollars

Cows, calves, and oxen, whether
    stall-fed or not, per head 5 now 25

Cobs. Cobs.

Sheep and goats, per ditto 2 — 7
Fowls, per dozen 1 — 6
Lemons and oranges, per thousand 1 — 5

Eggs, Per ditto 1 — 5
Dates, per quintal 4 — 8
Orange-trees, each 1 — 2
Figs, raisins, almonds, nuts, rhubarb,
    oil, honey, soap, olives,
    and red pepper, per quintal 2 — 12
Wheat, barley, oats, rice, and bean,
    per measure 1 — 6
Straw, by the nett 1/4 — 1
Pomegranates, amber-wood, %c., per quintal 1 — 4
Bees-wax and candles, per ditto 14 — 26
Ostrich feathers, per lb. 2 — 16
Ivory, copper, sandrach, chohob,
    and gum arabic, per quintal 5 — 15
Indigo, per ditto 1 — 10
Goat skins, per quintal 4 — 8
Beef ditto, per ditto 3 — 6
Lion and tiger ditto, each 4 — 12
Common tanned leather,per quintal 1 — 5
Morocco ditto free — 5
Wool and hemp, per quintal 3 — 6
All shoes and slippers,per hundred pair 4 — 10
Moorish caps, per ditto 4 — 10
Mats, each 1 — 5
Mules, ditto 10 — 50
Asses, ditto 5 — 10
Silk alhaiks, ditto 2 — 5
Haiks of other kinds, ditto 1 — 3

This is a correct translation of the agreement, and tariff, settled
eleven years ago, between the present Emperor Muley Solyman,
and the late Consul-general Mr. Matra. Having laid this before His
Excellency, I was so fortunate as to prevail on him to request the
Emperor to renew it, and to grant an increase of fresh provisions,
during the war, to the fleet off Cadiz, and to the garrison of Gibraltar.

It is impossible to doubt for a moment, at at whose instigation it
was that Ash-Ash behaved in this infamous manner. It is certainly

the interest of the French nation to prevent, if possible, our receiving supplies from Barbary; consequently we cannot wonder that every means should be employed to accomplish this end, and Ash-Ash is certainly the fittest instrument, from his hatred to the English: fortunately, however, he is not a free agent. My friend, and the friend of the English, the good Governor of this place, referred the whole to the Emperor, who has very satisfactorily adjusted every thing to our advantage, and the mortification of the French Consul, and his tool.

At the same time that His Excellency received the answer from the Emperor to the above-mentioned application, a letter arrived, requiring his immediate attendance at Fez; from which place you shall again hear from me.

LETTER X.

Depart from Larache with a little Army — Moorish military Salute — Numerous Villages — Customary Procession of the Inhabitants — Judicial Arrangements — River Beth resembles the Po — Herds of Camels — Arrive at Mequinez — French Falsehood again put down — Excellent Road from Mequinez — Fertility and Luxuriance of the adjacent Country — Procession to the Sanctuary of Sidy Edris — Multiplicity of Saints — Ceremony demonstrative of the Emperor's Favour — Take possession of my new Residence.

Fez, — — 1806.

In consequence of the dispatches received from the Emperor, we left Larache the same day. The Governor commands a territory of two hundred English miles. He put himself at the head of his troops, which amounted to six thousand cavalry, divided into squadrons, distinguished by their respective standards. There were in his train, besides, a prodigious number of mules, some carrying field equipage and provisions, others the treasures, consisting of the collected taxes, and presents for the Emperor.

This little army moved on in tolerably good order and discipline. It was preceded by an officer at the head of a small corps, doing the duty of a Quarter-master-general. We were met on our way by several officers, with small detachments of soldiers, under the government of His Excellency. The Moorish mode of saluting attracted my attention; when on a level in point of rank, the officers embrace each other, and then kiss the back of their own hand; but in saluting a superior, they kiss the hem of his garment; upon which he presents his hand, and they salute it. I assure you, they do all this with considerable grace.

In passing through villages (which in this part are very numerous, and formed of a much greater collection of tents than those described in a former letter), we were received by a great concourse of men, women, and children, shouting, and making a noise exactly resembling the whoop of the North American savages. I was informed, that this was their usual mode of expressing their joy and mirth, on all great and solemn occasions. A venerable Moor, the chief of the surrounding villages, accompanied by the military and civil officers, and by the principal inhabitants, advanced to kiss the garment of His Excellency: this ceremony was closed by a train of women, preceded by an elderly matron, carrying a standard of colours, made of various fillets of silk; and by a young one of great beauty, supporting on her head a bowl of fresh milk, which she presented, first to the Governor (or, as he is otherwise called, the Sheik), then to me, and afterwards to all the officers. This ceremony is always performed by the prettiest young woman of the village; and it not unfrequently happens, that her beauty captivates the affections of the great men (sometimes even the Emperor), and she becomes the legitimate and favourite wife.

When we arrived at any village, His Excellency halted to receive the report of the commanding officer; and to inquire if any murder, robbery, or other crimes, militating against the laws and constitution of the empire, had been perpetrated. This excellent man patiently listened to all the complaints made to him; and after hearing both parties with the greatest impartiality, he ordered such delinquents as stood fairly convicted to be punished by imprisonment, or fine, according to the nature of their offences. At one place where he held a court of justice, he received information of a band of assassins who had lately committed several murders and highway robberies, and had violated many young women, whom they afterwards destroyed. By this prompt and judicious arrangement, they were all secured, and brought before him. He ordered them to be dragged in the rear of his troops to Fez; there to receive whatever punishment the Emperor might think fit to award them.

We performed our route by short and easy stages, on a road which is perfectly level, and very different from those between Tetuan or Tangiers and Larache. We generally halted about two o'clock in the afternoon, and encamped; struck tents again at four in the morning, and then moved on regularly without noise or confusion.

On approaching the river *Beth*, we halted, to allow the baggage to cross, which was expeditiously conveyed in a large ferry-boat; the horses and mules were obliged to swim over, a spectacle curious and diverting enough. I passed over with the Governor; after which the boat went backwards and forwards till the whole of the troops were transported across the river, when we encamped, the side which we had quitted being occupied by another little army, headed by the Governor of another district. The two opposite camps had much the appearance of two hostile armies previous to a battle.

This river very much resembles the *Po* in Italy, and is perfectly navigable. On each side are immense fields of corn and rice, intersected by tracts of waste land covered with broom and heath, and spots of pasture-land on which large droves of camels graze. To prevent the camels from straying, they have one of their fore legs bent at the first joint, and tied up: they are attended by boys, who take them out early in the morning, and at night bring them back to the tents, before which each camel takes his place as regularly as our cows do in their stalls.

The next morning we reached a castle, and a ruinous walled town, occupied by soldiers, and slaves, who look after the herds of mules belonging to the Emperor. It is situated on a hill, whence I had a prospect of the immense plain we had first traversed, upon which not a single tree is to be seen.

About noon, on the sixth day, we approached a lofty mountain, which terminated this extensive plain, and formed the commencement of a chain of high hills, which we ascended and descended successively, and at length descried the large and populous city of Mequinez: we passed by a long aqueduct, a remnant of ancient architecture, and several Roman ruins, and reached one of the great gates of the town, where we were met by a strong detachment of soldiers commanded by the Governor, who, after the salutations and ceremonies usual on such occasions, escorted us to the palace of Eslawee, the Governor of Larache, where I was kindly received and most hospitably entertained by all his relations and friends.

On the morning after our arrival at Mequinez, an express arrived from the Emperor with an answer to a representation which I had made concerning the loss of a French privateer on the coast of Barbary; I had sent it at the same time with that respecting the tariff, and expected the answers together. The affair was this: a French privateer attempted to board several of our transports, laden with bullocks, from Tangiers for Gibraltar; but had scarcely succeeded with one, when the Confounder gun-brig, which was appointed to convoy them, came unobserved, within pistol-shot, and after an obstinate engagement of two hours the Frenchman ran on shore, and went to pieces immediately under the Moorish battery. This was considered, by the French Consul and his party, as an open violation of neutrality, and also a gross insult to His Imperial Majesty; and as such it was represented to him by Governor *Ash-Ash*, seconded by a letter from the French Consul, and supported by all his partisans. On our part, the statement was founded on simple facts, which perfectly satisfied the Emperor, and Governor *Ash-Ash* received a severe reprimand, accompanied by the remark, that His Imperial Majesty regretted the English had been so passive on this occasion, and that his subjects did not exterminate every Frenchman that presumed to land on his shores without his permission. You will feel assured that this additional triumph on our part gave me no small satisfaction.

My good friend Eslawee obtained leave likewise, to repose himself and his army for three days in his native place. This condescension was esteemed as an excellent omen. At the conclusion of the appointed time, we set off for this our ultimate destination. The road from Mequinez to Fez is excellent, extending along a pleasant and spacious plain, encompassed by high mountains, and intersected by small rivers, over which are stone bridges. These rivers are divided into several branches, which are again subdivided by the inhabitants, and carried in canals to water their lands. The prospect of the country is every where luxuriant in the extreme, and continually presents the most interesting objects. A scattered ruin, a large village, a meandering river, or a fine natural cascade, vineyards, woods, corn-fields, meadows, and saints' houses, surrounded by beautiful gardens and shrubberies, all lying in endless variety, formed the most picturesque landscapes.

As we left our quarters at Mequinez rather late, we encamped at eight o'clock in the evening at the opening of the plain I have just described. The next morning we set off much earlier than usual, but had not proceeded far when our progress was interrupted by a prodigious multitude of people, who pressed forward with such eagerness, that we were obliged to stand aside, and allow them to pass. Men, on horseback and on foot, women, and children, formed a procession which extended as far as the eye could reach. They were advancing in several divisions, each division preceded by a man bearing a standard, and by a band of music (if the horrible discord produced by their instruments could be dignified with the name of music), the people accompanying the band with their voices, shouting, bawling, and bellowing their national songs with the greatest vehemence.

These people were on their way to visit the sanctuary of *Sidy Edris*, the founder of Mahometanism in this country: it stands on the mountain *Zaaron*, at the western side of the plain of Fez, and near the city of Mequinez. Close to the sanctuary is a village, the inhabitants of which are held in the highest veneration, their huts and tents being consecrated to the Mahometan devotion, and, as well as the sanctuary, forming asylums for malefactors, which are never violated even by the Emperor. After this visit to the sanctuary, they attend an annual meeting, where they feast for three days, amusing themselves with dancing, fighting with wild beasts, and committing all kinds of excess in the ancient Bacchanalian style.

Formerly saints sprang up in Barbary like mushrooms. A Moor, seized in the night with a slight fit of insanity, was considered in the morning as a new saint, and as such he was revered, and his name added to their list of saints. In consequence of this, he was permitted to do whatever his fancy directed, without suffering the smallest molestation. Hence many worthless wretches feigned madness, in order that they might, with impunity, gratify their avaricious and revengeful passions, or their violent and ungovernable lust. The number of these impostors a few years back was incredible, and they literally held sovereign rule, from their numbers and great influence over this superstitious and fanatic people; but since the accession of Muley Solyman to the throne of Morocco, their influence and their numbers have considerably decreased. The country has been in a great measure swept and cleansed of imposters and other profligate persons, and the rest approach more and more towards a tolerable degree of civilization, under his paternal care and example. His chief study and attention appear to be directed to the welfare and happiness of his people.

We received no further interruptions; but reached this place on the 26th of April. On approaching the walls of the imperial palace, His Excellency formed his little army into a line of two deep. They fired a *feu de joie* with great precision and correctness. This done, they filed off to the place allotted for our encampment. Shortly after, two black slaves arrived from the palace, with a large bowl of fresh milk, and several cakes of bread, which were presented with much ceremony to His Excellency the Sheik, and received by him with marks of the most profound respect. This compliment was also paid to me, and to all his officers. This ceremony in Barbary, indicates that the person so honoured is a friend and favourite at the court of Morocco. The other Governors, with the exception of three, received the same honour, successively as they assembled on the plains of Fez, to be afterwards reviewed by the Emperor at the anniversary celebration of the birth of Mahomet. The three disgraced Governors were arrested the next day, thrown into prison, and condemned to remain there at the pleasure of the Emperor. Their whole property, amounting, as I am told, to several hundred thousand dollars, was confiscated.

My friend finding himself thus perfectly secure, appeared in high spirits, and proceeded to the palace to prostrate himself before his sovereign. He was received with every mark of the highest approbation and favour. At his return to the camp, he came to me with a smiling countenance, and related the flattering reception he had met with. He then informed me, that the Emperor had given orders, that a convenient house should be immediately provided for me, and that an officer of the household was coming to conduct me to my new habitation. This officer arrived while we were talking, and I followed him to my place of residence, which I found exceedingly neat and commodious. This I continue to occupy, and am furnished abundantly with all the delicacies which the city of Fez affords.

I have exceeded the bounds of moderation in this letter already, and must therefore postpone my introduction till my next.

LETTER XI.

Imperial Review of eighty thousand Cavalry — The Palace — Introduction to the Emperor — Visit the Seraglio — Beauty of the Sultana — Her Indisposition — Her Influence over the Emperor — His Person described.

Fez, — — 1806.

Late in the evening of the day of my arrival, I was visited at my house by an officer, who informed me that his royal master would review his troops the following morning, and that, if I chose to be present, I must repair to the palace precisely at four o'clock.

I was there exactly at the time, and in a few minutes the Emperor appeared, mounted on a beautiful white horse, attended by an officer of state, holding over him a large damask umbrella, most elegantly embroidered, and followed by all his great officers, body-guards, and a numerous band of music. He was greeted with huzzas in the Moorish style by the populace, and received at all the gates and avenues of the town with a general discharge of artillery and small arms, the people falling upon their knees in the dust as he passed. The streets were covered with mats, and the road, as far as the plain where the troops were drawn out, was strewed with all kinds of flowers.

The army was formed into a regular street of three deep on each side, each corps distinguished by a standard; it extended to a great length, through the immense plain of Fez, and presented a grand military spectacle. There were not less than eighty thousand cavalry. This review was finished in six hours, and His Imperial Majesty was so much pleased with the steady, orderly, and soldierlike appearance of his troops, that he commanded a horse to be given to each of the officers, and an additional suit of clothes and six ducats more than is customary to the men. No other exercise was performed on this occasion, than charging, firing off their pieces, and priming and loading at full gallop, by alternate divisions. Thus an incessant fire was kept up during the day.

The ground being perfectly level and good, no accident occurred. The dress of the Moorish army differs very little from that of the people. The officers are distinguished by their turbans, from the privates, who wear red caps. They are considered most excellent horsemen, and appeared to be supplied with very fine young horses, and well appointed. I can say but little of the infantry and artillery of His Imperial Majesty, not having had an opportunity of seeing them assemble in any sort of exercise. The cavalry are unquestionably most capital marksmen, and very capable of annoying and harassing and checking the progress of an invading army. The men are stout, strong, and robust, accustomed to a continual state of warfare, and, from their simple and moderate manner of living, fully adequate to sustain the fatigues and privations of the most arduous campaign.

In the Moorish army there is a prodigious number of blacks, who are reckoned very loyal, and perfectly devoted to the Emperor. This accounts for so many black governors being at the head of the most important districts and provinces of Barbary,

I returned very late from the review, and had scarcely dined when a messenger came to request my early attendance the following morning, to be presented to His Imperial Majesty. I repaired betimes to the palace, which is an immense pile of buildings, enclosed by a strong wall and a large deep ditch. It has four great gates, plated, both on the outside and in, with sheets of iron. I entered the front gate, and by a covered way reached a spacious court, surrounded by a piazza, under which several field-pieces and small mortars were placed. Here I was met by Sidy Ameth, a black officer, who acts as master of the ceremonies, and lord in waiting. He received me with great politeness, and conducted me, through another gate and covered way, to a second square more spacious than the first. In the centre was a most beautiful white marble basin, into which played a fountain of water clear as crystal. Over it was a kind of rotunda, supported by columns of elegant black marble. This superb square is paved with small pieces of marble, intermixed with pebbles of various colours, in the mosaic style. It is formed by four wings of the building. The front wing, exclusive of its magnificent entrance, contains several apartments and waiting-rooms, occupied by the great officers of state; the right, the library, and the treasury of the Emperor; the left, a superb mosque, and a school-room for the use of the Emperor's children, where they are taught to read and write, and study the Alcoran; and finally, the back, the great hall of audience, in which His Imperial Majesty was seated cross-legged upon a kind of couch, under a crimson velvet canopy, most beautifully decorated with figured work in gold.

I was introduced by Sidy Ameth; and after making my obsequious reverence, I stood at a great distance, waiting the Imperial commands, when His Majesty was graciously pleased to order me, by signs, to draw near, and then, by means of an interpreter, he informed me, that, in consequence of the good I had done his subjects during my residence at Larache, he had long been anxious to see and consult me. He desired me to ask any favours I chose, either for myself or my country, and they should be granted immediately. I thanked His Majesty for his condescension, and then presented him with a patent pistol, with seven barrels, which he examined very attentively in every part, and appeared highly pleased with its construction.

He commanded the hall to be cleared, and in a very friendly and familiar way told me the nature of his complaint; after which he summoned the chief eunuch, and desired me to follow him to the seraglio, to prescribe for his favourite Sultana, who was seriously indisposed. On leaving the hall of audience, we turned to the left, and arrived at a gate, which terminated the piazza on the right side of the square. Through this gate we entered a large passage, paved with marble; on each side were marble benches, upon which the eunuch informed me, the inferior eunuchs and the female attendants of the seraglio slept. This passage conducted us to another square, on the right of which is the Imperial bath. It is almost impossible to form an idea of the elegance and convenience of this structure, which is used only by the Emperor.

Adjoining the bath is a refectory, which is constantly supplied with every kind of refreshment. The other sides of this square contained the apartments of two or more ladies of His Imperial Majesty. It would be tedious to enumerate the several squares through which I passed; they differ only in splendour and magnificence, according to the rank and taste of those ladies to whom they belong: they all communicate from one piazza to another, by means of passages, such as I have described. I was extremely indebted to my black conductor for giving me an opportunity of seeing the whole of the seraglio; for I returned by a much less circuitous route than that by which I went, the apartments of the Sultana being just behind the Imperial bath. But where shall I find words to give you an adequate idea of their lovely inhabitant? Conceive every thing that is beautiful, and you may possibly arrive near the mark. She is rather below the middle size, exquisitely fair, and well proportioned. When I first saw her, she was in a very doubtful state, and I reported accordingly to the Emperor; he was sensibly affected, and besought me to exert my utmost skill, to preserve a life of so much value to him. Happily, my efforts have been crowned with success, and I hope a very short time will restore her to perfect health. She controls him in every thing, and is considered, from her absolute dominion over him, as the fountain of all favours.

The gardens of the seraglio are beautifully laid out by Europeans, and contain several elegant pavilions and summer-houses, where the ladies take tea and recreate themselves; baths, fountains, and solitary retreats for those inclined to meditation: in short, nothing is wanting to render this a Complete terrestrial paradise, but liberty, the deprivation of which must embitter every enjoyment.

Muley Solyman, the present Emperor, is about thirty-eight years of age, in height about six feet two inches, of a tolerably fair complexion, with remarkably fine teeth, large dark eyes, aquiline nose, and black beard; the *tout ensemble* of his countenance noble and majestic. He governs Barbary with discretion and moderation; in the distribution of justice, or in rewarding his subjects, he is just and impartial; in his private conduct no less pious and exemplary, than, in his public capacity, firm and resolute, prompt and courageous. In my next letter I shall give you a brief account of the succession of Sovereigns from the time of *Edris* to the present reigning family.

LETTER XII.

Succession of the Sovereigns from their Founder to the present Emperor.

Fez, — — 1806.

Edris; the founder of Mahometanism in Barbary, was succeeded by his posthumous son, *Edris the Second*, who founded the first monarchy, after that of Mahomet, in these regions; and it was called the Kingdom of the West. The family of Edris continued to reign for about a hundred and fifty years; but was disturbed, during the tenth century, by several intestine divisions, excited by a crowd of usurpers, which terminated in the total extinction of the Edrissites.

The tribe of Mequinici seized on several provinces, and founded, on the ruins of the ancient, the present city of Mequinez.

Abu-Tessifin, a Maraboot, or Monk, taking advantage of the divisions which convulsed these countries, and above all of the credulity of this fickle people, sent several of his disciples to preach and excite the multitude to revolt, under the pretext of recovering their liberties. This great impostor was the chief of the tribe of *Lamthunes*, surnamed *Morabethoon*, on account of the extreme rigour with which they observed the forms of the new religion.

This tribe resided between Mount Atlas and the Desert. The Moors being weary of their Arabian rulers, flocked in crowds to the standard of Tessefin, who soon found himself at the head of a large army, by means of which he conquered, many provinces, and established himself Sovereign of Mauritania.

He was succeeded by his son *Joseph-Ben-Tessefin*, who in 1086 finished the city of Morakesh, or Morocco, which his father had begun, and there fixed his seat of government. In 1097 he seized on the kingdom of Fez, and united it to that of Morocco: he also joined his forces to those of the Mahometans in Spain, and conquered the city of Seville, subdued all Andalusia, Grenada, and Murcia, penetrated as far as Cordova, and defeated the army of Alphonso VI. of Spain. After which he returned, loaded with spoils, to Morocco, where he died. He was succeeded by his son *Aly*, who likewise passed over into Spain, but was defeated and slain by Alphonso at the battle of Moriella.

His son *Brahem*, an indolent prince, and much addicted to pleasure, was proclaimed King of Morocco. His profligacy favoured the ambitious projects of a Mahometan preacher, named *Mahomet Abdallah*. This impostor assumed the name of *Mahedi, Commander of the Faithful*, and drew a host of people to his standard. In the course of his mission, he met another preacher, at the head of a multitude of followers, who also styled himself *Mahedi*, or *the Prophet* expected at the end of ages.

These two adventurers, consulting their mutual interest, coalesced, and having completely succeeded in seducing the people, by projects of reformation, *Abdallah* was proclaimed King of Morocco, and *Abdul-Momen*, the other imposter, General of the Faithful. This having effected the destruction of Brahem, he contrived to dispatch his colleague so privately as to avoid the imputation of being accessary to his death, and succeeded him in the sovereignty. He demolished all the palaces and mosques of the Kings in Morocco, and laid the greater part of that city in ruins, it having shut its gates against him when, he presented himself before it; and he destroyed the young son of Brahem with his own hands. He afterwards, however, rebuilt Morocco, and died in 1155, in possession of the sovereign power.

He was succeeded by his son Joseph, who passed over into Spain, and engaging with the armies of the Kings of Portugal and Leon, he was killed by a fall from his horse. His son *Abu-Jacob*, surnamed *Almonsor* the Invincible, assumed the government, suppressed the divisions that distracted the country, and, rendered himself so powerful and formidable, that the Mahometan Kings in Spain elected him as their supreme ruler. After performing numberless gallant exploits, he disappeared on a sudden, as some assert, to perform the pilgrimage to Mecca; but it is most probable, he was secretly murdered and buried by the descendants of Abdallah. His son ascended the throne, but died in a very short time of grief, in consequence of his losses in Spain. He was the last King of this family.

Abdallah, the Governor of Fez, of the tribe of Benimecius, usurped the crown of his master. Of his successors, the only prince who took part in the Mahometan wars in Spain was *Abul Hassen*, who conquered Gibraltar, and built the fort which still retains the name of the *Moorish Castle*. He was dethroned and assassinated by his son, *Abul Hassen*, a ferocious and ambitious tyrant, who left a son, named *Abu-Said*, of a very depraved character, in whose reign Ceuta, after a long siege, was taken by Don John, King of Portugal.

These usurpers were completely extirpated by the house of Merini, which family in its turn was overcome by *Muley Mahomet*, a Xeriffe of the same tribe, who seized the reins of government. His successors did not long enjoy the fruit of their usurpation, but were most dreadfully disturbed by a series of revolutions and murders, fomented and perpetrated by the mountaineers, a resolute, ferocious, and restless people, who, after raising the various parts of the country in arms one against the other, and subjecting them to all the calamities of civil war, cruelly butchered *Muley Achmet*, the last of the sons of *Muley Sidan* and proclaimed their chief, *Crom-el-Hadgy*, a bloodthirsty ruffian, of low birth, and eminent in cruelties, in his stead. This tyrant, to secure his new acquisition, inhumanly massacred all the male descendants of the Xeriffes. He soon became the object of universal detestation, and was poignarded by his Sultana on the day of marriage. She was of the family of the Xeriffes, and consented to marry him, only that she might have a better opportunity of sacrificing him to her revenge, for the murder of her family.

After the tragical end of the descendants of the Xeriffes, these countries, but more especially the province of Tafilet, experienced all the horrors of famine and pestilence, for several years. The people of Tafilet considered it as a judgment from their Prophet for their injustice; and, to appease him, they made a pilgrimage to Mecca, and easily prevailed on a Xeriffe, a descendant of Mahomet, named *Muley Aly*, who resided in a town near Medina, to accompany them back to this country. In the mean time, the seasons having become more genial, the harvests were so abundant, that this credulous and superstitious people attributed the change entirely to the arrival of the pious Xeriffe. He was unanimously proclaimed King of Tafilet, by the name of *Muley Xeriffe*; and as such acknowledged by the other provinces, with the exception of Morocco and its environs, which were then in the possession of *Crom-el-Hadgy*, who having ended his career in the manner described, was soon followed by his son; and the ancient families who had ruled the empire being completely extinct, the new King of Tafilet, from his birth, religion, and the public election, was confirmed the legitimate Sovereign of the whole county.

Muley Xeriffe was the founder of the dynasty of *Fileli*, from which the present reigning family is descended. This country, totally exhausted by divisions and civil wars, acquired the enjoyments of peace and plenty, during the reign of this prince, who resided at Tafilet, and caused the Governors, who were entrusted with provinces, to rule with equity. He made it his whole study to render this fickle and turbulent people happy; the latter part of his reign was perfectly undisturbed, and his death was universally and justly lamented. He was succeeded by his eldest son, who was proclaimed, without the disturbances usual on those occasions, by the name of *Muley Mahomet*.

This prince, equally just and pious with his father, reigned for some time very peaceably; and from his exemplary conduct would have continued to do so to his death, to the increasing prosperity of his subjects, but for his brother, *Muley Arshid*, an ambitious prince, who, endowed with an intelligent mind, equal to the vast project he had in contemplation, raised a rebellion, with a view to seize on the sovereign power. At the head of a numerous party, in a pitched battle, he was however defeated, and taken prisoner, by his brother *Muley Mahomet*. But he recovered his liberty, by the aid of a negro slave, whom he rewarded by striking off his head at the very instant he had enabled the monster to recover his liberty.

After wandering about for some time, stirring up the minds of the people to revolt, Muley Arshid fled to the mountains of Rif, where he offered his services to the Sovereign of those districts, who, unfortunately discovering the abilities of the stranger, confided to him the administration of his territories, when, after having by stratagem and prodigality gained the troops and the people to his interests, he dethroned and inhumanly butchered his royal benefactor. He then defeated his brother *Mahomet*, and closely besieged him in Tafilet, whence that good prince died of grief. To enumerate the bloody exploits of this prince would extend my letter to a volume; suffice it therefore to say, that his reign was short, and the remembrance of it never to be effaced. He died in 1672 of a fractured skull, in consequence of a fall from his horse.

He was succeeded by his brother *Muley Ishmael*, who distinguished himself by some brave actions; and his reign would have formed a grand epoch in the history of this country, had he not stained it by a succession of tyranny and cruelties, too shocking to dwell upon. He died in 1727 at the advanced age of eighty-one, leaving behind him a numerous offspring. This prince, in order to ensure his despotic and arbitrary power, contrived to form a regular army of foreign soldiers, which he effected, partly from the negro families, then settled in Barbary, but principally from a vast number of blacks which he obtained from the coast of Guinea.

Muley-Achmet-Daiby, one of the numerous sons of Ishmael, ascended the throne of Morocco, and, after reigning two years, died of a dropsy. His successor, *Muley Abdallah*, by far surpassed all his predecessors in point of vices and cruelty. His conduct was so flagrant, that he was deposed no less than six times, but as often re-elected. Amidst civil wars, divisions, and devastations, the plague again made its appearance, and committed the same dreadful ravages as in the reign of *Ishmael*. Being reinstated for the sixth time, *Abdallah* took advantage of the troubles occasioned by this terrible disease, to excite divisions among his negro soldiers, by whose power alone he had suffered all his humiliations. Vast numbers of this warlike race fell the victims of his treachery, and he succeeded in reducing them so low, that they were no longer a subject of dread to him. Having thus freed himself of all cause of restraint, he recovered his power, and, if possible, plunged deeper than ever into the gulf of iniquity; and each succeeding day was stained with crimes of the blackest hue. The only sentiments with which he inspired his unhappy people were those of terror and disgust. At length, worn out with age, he died at Fez in 1757; and was succeeded by his son *Sidi Mahomet*, who had begun to reform several abuses, during the latter part of his father's reign, when he had been entrusted with the government of Morocco.

This prince, the father of the present Emperor, was endowed with an intelligent mind, and possessed nothing of the barbarian. His political views, and excellent regulations, soon restored the order of things. He directed all his care to the welfare of his people, both at home and abroad; he concluded, and renewed, several advantageous commercial treaties, with England, France, Spain, Portugal, Sweden, Denmark, and Holland, with all of whom he maintained a good understanding till 1777; when, gained over by the courts of France and Spain, he broke the treaty with England, and refused to supply Gibraltar with fresh provisions. He appointed officers of the strictest integrity, and of moderate and resolute characters, to the government of his provinces; and the whole period of his reign was exempt from those horrible cruelties which had almost invariably disgraced the sceptres of his predecessors. He died at an advanced age, at *Rabat*, on the 11th of April 1790.

After the old Emperor's death, the states of Barbary became convulsed by the civil discords, attended with great effusion of bloody occasioned by Sidi Mahomet's numerous sons, who severally aspired to the crown. The contest was for a long time doubtful and bloody; but at length, Muley Yezid was proclaimed Emperor, by a powerful party. As the whole country was up in arms, he had to combat with many difficulties in establishing himself on the throne. He was no sooner confirmed in his power, than he exercised it with uncommon cruelty towards his captives. Under the idea of striking terror into the minds of his subjects, by the force of example, and deterring them from revolting again, he inflicted the most dreadful punishment on those who had opposed his authority; some he caused to be hung up by the feet, and suffered to perish for want of sustenance; others, to be crucified at the gates of the city; and several high priests, and officers of state, he deprived of the blessing of sight.

But his cruelty and inhumanity did not rest here. In the above proceedings he might possibly urge in palliation a regard to his personal safety, and the possession of a crown which he held by so precarious a tenure as the caprice of a multitude, who might wrest it from him with as little scruple as they had bestowed it, if not awed by some terrible example; but where shall we seek an excuse for his execrable barbarity to the poor Jews in his dominions, whom he ordered to be massacred, without distinction? The carnage was most horrible; and the property of this persecuted people was indiscriminately plundered by their rapacious murderers. Six young

Jewesses, who ventured to intercede for their unhappy fathers and relations, were burned alive. My blood runs cold at the idea of such depravity; and I shrink, from the reflection that our own history will furnish us with annals, almost or fully as replete with horror as the one I am now relating.

It is not all surprising that such unjustifiable cruelty should kindle disgust in the minds of those who were not totally divested of the feelings of humanity. Several of his provinces rebelled, but he successively reduced them to obedience; and in the last battle which he fought, before the city of Morocco, and gained, he was severely wounded. The rebel army was surrounded, and defeated with great slaughter. *Muley Yezid* was carried to the castle, and his wound dressed; but his treatment was so improper, that, after lingering a few days in the most excruciating torture, he died in 1794.

The present Emperor, *Muley Solyman*, was the youngest prince, and lived retired in the city of Fez, assiduously occupied in studying the Alcoran and the laws of the empire, in order to qualify himself for the office of high-priest, which he was intended to fill. From this retreat he was called by the priests, the highest in repute as saints, in the neighbourhood of Fez, and a small party of the Moorish militia, and by them prevailed upon to come forward as a candidate for the crown, in opposition to his three brothers, who were waging war with each other, at the head of numerous forces. In the midst of this anarchy and confusion, the young prince was proclaimed Emperor at Fez, by the name of *Muley Solyman*; and having collected a strong force, aided by the counsels of a number of brave and experienced officers, he advanced to Mequinez, which he reduced, after two successive pitched battles. This place was defended by one of his brothers, who shortly after acknowledged him as Emperor, joined him, and brought over to his interests a great number of friends and partisans. He served Solyman faithfully ever after, which enabled him to withstand the united forces of his two other brothers. At length, owing to the little harmony that prevailed in the armies of his competitors, he effected his purpose. Taking advantage of their increasing animosity, he advanced towards Morocco, fighting and conquering the whole way. He entered the capital in triumph, after a general and decisive battle; and he was again proclaimed Emperor.

This brave young prince had now reduced Barbary entirely under his sway, with the exception of the kingdom of Tangiers. Thither the two unfortunate princes retired, in order to make a last and desperate stand; but after a variety of struggles, to regain some degree of ascendancy, one was compelled to solicit the protection of the Dey of Algiers, and the other was taken prisoner, and banished to a remote province.

From that period, the Emperor has dedicated the whole of his time and pursuits to the amelioration of his people's condition, by improving his financial resources, and appointing over his provinces, mild and humane Governors, whom he strictly superintends, occasionally deposing such as have deviated from his orders, and often inflicting upon these his representatives the most severe corporal punishments, previous to their imprisonment for life.

LETTER XIII.

Responsibility of the Governors — Empire beautiful and productive — Humane Efforts of the Emperor — Blind Submission to his Will — Great Number of Negroes naturalized — The Moors might be truly formidable. — Emperor's Brother — Fez divided into two Parts — Magnificent Mosques — Commercial Privileges — Indignities which Christians undergo — Singular Supply of Water — The Imperial Gardens — Propensity to defraud — Factories — Exports — Costume — Character — Manner of living — Domestic Vermin.

Fez.

Having extended my last letter to an unusual length, I broke off rather abruptly; I shall therefore resume the subject in this.

The Governors commanding large districts or provinces in Barbary, are answerable for the crimes and misdemeanors committed in their governments, if they fail to bring the offenders to public justice; consequently they impose very heavy fines on the community, to impel them to seize, and deliver to them, the murderer or robber. The sudden and frequent changes in the public offices keep the most powerful Governors in the empire in continual awe and depression; and the fear of being, in an instant, hurled from the height of prosperity to the lowest abyss of adversity, usually prevents them from amassing great wealth, as it is sure to pass into the Emperor's treasury on their disgrace; and the same cause prevents the forming of dangerous cabals. Yet some of them contrive, during their short-lived administration, to squeeze from their wretched vassals as much money as they can, by every fraudful artifice and despotic violence. The sufferers murmur, and complain; but the government appears to wink at the oppression for a time, and reserves its dreadful vengeance till the annual review, on the plains of Fez, where the collected spoils of the cruel peculator are seized, and himself deposed, imprisoned, and the whole fruit of his rapine transferred to the royal treasury.

This empire is one of the most beautiful and fertile countries, perhaps in the world; but the despotism under which it has groaned, and the capricious humours of its former rulers, destroyed, and prevented the effects of industry; besides, the rapacity of the Sheiks, who are the Bashaws of the country, carried off every thing that labour could collect. The present Emperor is endeavouring to correct these abuses, and to bring about a reformation, which I am sure he will never effect, owing to the great influence of the priests and saints in these states. Although this monarch is humane and impartial, and possesses nothing of the ferocious character of his predecessors, yet seldom a day passes without some executions.

The people regard their Emperor as a god upon earth, and revere him as a descendant of their great prophet. All his commands, right or wrong, just or unjust, they consider as the decrees of Heaven. A blind obedience to the will of their Sovereign, is inculcated in the minds of their youth, more as a matter of religion than of state; and the Emperor may put as many of his subjects to death as he deems expedient, without assigning any other motive for so doing than secret inspiration. When at war with any Christian prince, it is considered as a war of religion, and the Moors who fall in the field of battle, are accounted martyrs.

The number of negroes that have been imported into this country, and are now settled in these states, is astonishing. The amount is little less than three hundred thousand. The Emperor's body-guard, which consists of eighteen thousand horsemen, is chiefly composed of negroes, who enjoy every privilege that despotic power can confer, and are ready upon all occasions to enforce the royal mandate.

The great schools for the Moorish gentry are the chanceries of the Bashaws, where the young men learn the arts of dissimulation and duplicity in the greatest perfection, and become, very, early such great adepts in these valuable acquirements, that in my opinion they are fully able to cope with Monsieur Talleyrand, and the best politicians at the court of St. Cloud. They are very dexterous also in the art of temporizing with an enemy, and deluding him by a thousand little expedients. It is therefore fortunate for Europe, that the Moors are so indolent a set of people; for the immense power this empire might have; were it peopled by an industrious and ambitious race of men, would render it the most formidable in the world.

I shall now return to my own affairs, from the period at which they were left off in a former letter. The Emperor had requested me to report to him, personally, every morning, the state of his favourite Sultana; I therefore waited upon him regularly at five o'clock, and was extremely happy that I was enabled to make the report more welcome each day. After this visit to His Imperial Majesty, I daily paid my devoirs to the blind prince, the only remaining brother of the Emperor now in Barbary, and who took no part in the disputes of former times; and I then called upon the great officers of state.

Finding the Sultana in such a fair way of recovery, the Emperor dismissed his Governors to their respective provinces, and removed his court to Mequinez, his favourite summer residence, leaving me here, to complete the cure of the Sultana, and to attend several of his subjects, who stand high in his favour, in the lower town of Fez. As the attendance required by my patients does not occupy the whole of my time, I employ my leisure in observing such things as appear most worthy of remark.

The town (or rather *towns* of Fez, this city being divided into two distinct parts, the one called Upper, the other Lower Fez) is the capital of the kingdom of that name, and is supposed to contain about three hundred thousand inhabitants, besides foreigners of their own persuasion. There are upwards of five hundred mosques:

one of them in particular, which was built by Edris the Second, and in which his remains were deposited, is magnificent beyond description, and is about a mile and a half in circumference. There is another very little inferior to this, which was erected by the Arabs of Caiwan, and called *Carubin*. The other mosques have been constructed since. To most of the mosques are annexed several colleges, religious schools, and hospitals for the pilgrims who visit this place, for, in point of holiness, it is considered as next to Mecca and Medina.

The lower town of Fez was built by Edris the Second, about the end of the eighth century, and is taken notice of by Pliny under the name of *Volubilis*. According to that author, and others, this city ranked amongst the principal inland towns of Mauritania, and was a Roman colony. It is a place of considerable trade; the inhabitants are mostly freed men, engaged in commerce, and reputed to be very opulent and industrious; they have purchased a charter, by which they ensure a kind of independence, and are totally unmolested in their traffic; in short, there are great privileges attached to this town, which are not to be met with in any other part of Barbary. The lower town is almost entirely surrounded by hills, which are highly cultivated, and abound with vineyards, and gardens producing most exquisite fruits.

Upper Fez is situated on one of the highest of the hills which almost encircle the lower town, and contains the imperial palace and seraglio, several old palaces occupied by the sons of the Emperor, and the habitations of the principal officers in the household. Contiguous to these, is the inclosed town belonging solely to the Jews, who are about thirty thousand in number, having one hundred and fifty synagogues. On that part of the wall of the Jewish town which overlooks Lower Fez, are placed several heavy pieces of ordnance, which, in case of an insurrection in the latter, would very soon demolish it: as the lower town is by much the most populous and extensive, this precaution may not be unnecessary. The Jewish town is commanded by an Alcaid, who cannot however shield its unfortunate inhabitants from oppression and insults. These people are obliged to walk barefooted through the Moorish streets; and they suffer the greatest outrages without a murmur, nay, some of them have been actually murdered in the act of selling their goods to the

Moors. No Christian is allowed to appear publicly in the streets of Fez, without a special permission from the Emperor, and a military escort.

These towns are supplied with water in a most singular manner from a river, called *Rasalema*, which takes its source in a valley near the road to Mequinez. It issues from a rock, about eight or ten feet above the ground, in a stream, that, from the form of the valley through which it runs, appears a continued waterfall. It is conveyed into the Emperor's garden by means of a large wheel, about twenty-five feet in diameter, round which, at regular distances, are small buckets, which, as the wheel goes round, are alternately filled, and emptied into a reservoir at the top of the wall of the garden. From the reservoir the water is also conveyed to the upper and lower towns by aqueducts.

On the outside of one of the western gates of Upper Fez are the gardens of the Emperor, surrounded by a good stone wall, within which are a number of spacious walks, shaded by rows of tall trees, on each side, and intersected by parterres and grass-plots, on which are elegant pavilions, some in a pyramidical, others in a conical form, where the Emperor frequently retires, to take his repose, or to amuse himself with his courtiers. These pavilions are between thirty and forty feet in height, covered on the outside with varnished tiles of different colours, and contain three and sometimes four neat apartments, furnished in the most simple style imaginable, having in general nothing more than a carpet, several couches, a few arm-chairs, a table, a clock, and a tea-equipage of china. The cornices round the walls of these apartments are embellished with passages from the Koran, and other Arabic sentences, carved in cedar-wood.

The propensity to cheating, so prevalent in all Barbary, is no where so notorious as in the lower town of Fez; and the Europeans who trade with the Moorish merchants here must employ the same means as themselves, or submit to be most flagitiously imposed upon.

I have visited several manufactories of carpets, mats, silk, linen, and leather, of which the merchants export great quantities. I have also seen some beautifully embroidered shawls, scarfs, and sword-knots, of the manufacture of this country. Their exports besides are, elephants' teeth, ostrich feathers, copper, tin, wool, hides, honey, wax, dates, raisins, olives, almonds, gum-arabic, and sandrach. They carry on a considerable trade, by caravans, to Mecca and Medina, the inland regions of Africa, and to the farthermost parts of the coast of Guinea; from which last place they bring gold-dust, and a prodigious number of negroes, some of whom are destined to serve in the Emperor's armies; the rest are slaves in the Moorish houses and fields.

The dress of the Moors is composed of a linen shirt, over which they fasten a cloth or silk vestment with a sash, loose trowsers reaching to the knee, a white serge cloak, or capote, and yellow slippers: their arms and legs are quite bare. The principal people are distinguished by the fineness of their turbans, their linen shirts, and cloth or silk garments, which are richly embroidered with gold; when they go abroad, they cover this dress with an alhaik, differing in quality according to the circumstances of the wearer; and which they fold round them like a large blanket. They never move their turbans, but pull off their slippers, when they attend religious duties, or their Sovereign, or visit their relatives, friends, priests, or civil and military officers.

The Moorish gentry are clean in their persons, in their manners tolerably genteel and complaisant, far from being loquacious, though not prone to reflection. They possess an unbounded degree of duplicity and flattery; are perfectly strangers to the notions of truth and honour, promising a thing one day which they utterly deny the next. They are less irascible than many other nations; but when grossly injured, seek revenge in assassination. They are more vindictive than brave, more superstitious than devout, firmly attached to their ancient customs, and wholly averse to every kind of innovation.

The Moors, in general, are extremely fond of fruit and vegetables, which contribute very much to their contentment. The peasants eat meat only on certain great days. They are excessively dirty in their cooking, and the style of their dishes is not at all adapted to the taste of an Englishman. Their soups are made most intolerably hot with spices; and their favourite dish is *cous-ca-sou*, which appears to me to be prepared in the following manner: The meat and vegetables are laid alternately in a large bowl, and seasoned; then the whole is covered with fine wheaten flour, made into small grains, very like the Italian pastes. It is raised into the form of a pyramid, and I should imagine stewed, or rather steamed, as the outside remains perfectly white, which it would not were it baked. The whole of the inside, when brought to table, is mingled almost into one mass; the meat separating from the bones, without the smallest difficulty: it does not contain any gravy, and the Moors eat it by handsfull.

I generally live upon mutton and veal, both of which are very good: the bread and butter are excellent, but the latter will not keep more than twenty-four hours without becoming rancid. My greatest annoyance here is the infinite number of bugs and fleas, which infest me by day and night most intolerably.

LETTER XIV.

Fez – Debility of the Moors – Mosques – Antiquities, Roman, Carthaginian, and Saracen – Storks held in great Veneration – Baths – Bazars – Inhabitants – Residence – Menagerie – Marvellous Preservation of a Jew – Lions – Tigers – Leopards – Hyenas.

Fez, — —.

Considering the mildness of the climate, the uncommon fertility of the soil, the number of mineral waters, the fragrancy and salubrity of the air, one would imagine that the frame and constitution of a Moor cannot but be beautiful, strong, and healthy; yet, though the most handsome people of both sexes are to be met with in this great city, the number of miserable objects, the wretched victims of excessive early passions, is in a much larger proportion: it is shocking beyond description to meet them in every corner of the streets. I have visited a great many of these poor creatures, and found them in such a state, that decency obliges me to draw a veil over it.

The mosques of this town, which I have before mentioned as very numerous, are square buildings, and generally of stone; before the principal gate there is a court paved with white marble, with piazzas round, the roofs of which are supported by marble columns. In niches within these piazzas, the Moors perform their ablutions before they enter the mosques. Attached to each mosque is a tower, with three small open galleries, one above another, whence the people are called to prayer, not by a bell, but by an officer appointed for that duty. These towers, as well as the mosques, are covered with lead, and adorned with gilding, and tiles of variegated colours. No woman is allowed to enter the Moorish places of worship.

Several of the aqueducts, which were constructed by the Carthaginians and Romans, are still to be seen; and the ruins of amphitheatres, and other public buildings, are found in the town and neighbourhood of Fez: likewise many Saracen monuments of the most stupendous magnificence, which were erected under the Caliphs of Bagdad. The mosques and ruins are frequented by a great number of storks, which are very tame, and are regarded by the Moors as a kind of inferior saints.

The baths here are wonderfully well constructed for the purpose. Some of them are square buildings, but the greater part are circular, paved with black or white polished marble, and containing three rooms: the first for undressing and dressing, the second for the water, and in the third is the bath. Their manner of bathing is very curious: the attendant rubs the person with great force, then pulls and stretches the limbs, as if he meant to dislocate every joint. This exercise to these indolent people is very conducive to health.

The bazars in which the tradesmen have their shops, are very extensive. These shops are filled with all kinds of merchandise. In the centre of the town is a rectangular building, with colonnades, where the principal merchants attend daily to transact business.

The inhabitants of Fez are of a large muscular stature, fair complexion, with black beards and eyes; extremely amorous and jealous of their women, whom they keep strictly guarded. Their houses consist of four wings, forming a court in the centre, round which is an arcade, or piazza, with one spacious apartment on each side. The court is paved with square pieces of marble, and has a basin of the same in the centre, with a fountain. They keep their houses remarkably clean and neat; but all the streets of this immense town are narrow, very badly paved with large irregular stones, and most shockingly dirty. The tops of their houses, like those of Tetuan, and other towns in Barbary, are flat, for the purpose of recreation.

Among the remnants of several amphitheatres, there is one very nearly entire, which is kept in constant repair at the expense of the Emperor, and appropriated as a menagerie for lions, tigers, and leopards. As I was contemplating it the other day, I felt at a loss to account for this being kept in repair, while the others were suffered to moulder into dust, unheeded, excepting a very few, and those but partially prevented from sharing the general wreck. I had stood some time, thus employed, when I was suddenly interrupted in my meditations, by the sound of voices close behind me; on turning I perceived two Jews, one of whom I knew very well, from having given advice to some part of his family. I immediately inquired how it happened that the building before us was so carefully preserved from going to ruin, as happened to most of the others. He informed me, that it was a kind of menagerie for wild beasts. "It was the same in the time of the late Emperor," continued he; "and a very curious incident befell one of my brethren in that place." As the narrative was not merely very curious, but really wonderful, I cannot forbear sending you the substance of it; as to give it you in the very circuitous way it came to me, would be rather a tax upon your patience, particularly, as you may not be so destitute of resources of amusement, as, I confess, I was at that moment.

It appears, that Muley Yezid, the late Emperor, had a great and invincible antipathy to the Jews (indeed it was but too evident in the horrible transaction I mentioned in a former letter). An unfortunate Israelite, having incurred the displeasure of that prince, was condemned to be devoured by a ferocious lion, which had been purposely left without food for twenty-four hours: when the animal was raging with hunger, the poor Jew had a rope fastened round his waist, and in the presence of a great concourse of people was let down into the den; his supplications for mercy, and screams of terror, availing him nothing. The man gave himself up for lost, expecting every moment to be torn in pieces by the almost famished beast, who was roaring most hideously; he threw himself on the ground in an agony of mind, much better conceived than described. While in this attitude, the animal approached him, ceased roaring, smelt him two or three times, then walked majestically round him, and gave him now and then a gentle whisk with his tail, which seemed to signify that he might rise, as he would not hurt him; finding the man still continue motionless with fear, he retreated a few paces, and laid himself down like a dog. After a short time had elapsed, the Jew, recovering from his insensibility, and perceiving himself unmolested, ventured to raise himself up, and observing the noble animal couched, and no symptom of rage or anger in his countenance, he felt animated with confidence. In short, they became quite friendly, the lion suffering himself to be caressed by the Jew with the utmost tameness. It ended with the man being drawn up again unhurt, to the great astonishment of the spectators. A heifer was afterwards let down, and instantly devoured. You may be sure this story was too great a triumph on the part of the Israelites, to pass without a number of annotations and reflections from the narrator, all tending to prove the victory of their nation over the heathens. For my part, I could not help thinking that there was too much of the miraculous in it. However, I have often heard it asserted that the lion will never touch a man who is either dead, or counterfeits death; indeed here they tell me, that, unless pressed by hunger or rage, it never molests a man; and they assure me even that upon no account will these animals injure a woman, but, on the contrary, will protect her, when they meet her at a watering-place. This country abounds with lions, tigers, leopards, and hyenas, which sometimes make nocturnal visits to the villages, and spread desolation among the sheep and cattle.

LETTER XV.

Sudden Departure from Fez — Arrive at Mequinez — Attend the Emperor — Melancholy Catastrophe — Expedition against wild Beasts — Extensive Palaces — Seraglio — Visit a Haram — Founders of the City — A fortified Town — Inhabitants — Jewish Town — Rich Attire of the higher Orders — Numerous Market-places — Furniture — Saints' Houses — Imperial Field Sports — Pack of Greyhounds — Abundance of Game.

Mequinez.

No doubt, my dear D— —, you will be very much surprised to observe my letter dated from this place. I assure you I had not the most distant idea, when I wrote last, of removing so suddenly from Fez. On the evening of the same day that I dispatched my letter to you, as I was preparing for rest, an express arrived from the Emperor, begging me to repair hither without delay. Concluding that nothing less than life or death depended on my speedy arrival, I accordingly renounced the pleasures of the drowsy god for a very uneasy seat on the back of a mule, and at midnight set off for this place, leaving my baggage and attendants to follow in the morning. I rode very fast all night, and arrived here about nine o'clock the next day. When I dismounted, I was so extremely stiff, that it was with the utmost difficulty I could stand; I was most dreadfully fatigued, and stood in very great need of repose; but waving all selfish considerations, I thought only of being serviceable, and therefore lost no time in waiting on the Emperor. He received me in the kindest and most flattering manner, and expressed great pleasure at seeing me; but I found my patient's case not so very urgent as I had imagined; a few hours delay would not have endangered the life of any human being, and it would have saved *one*, some aching bones. However, after dispatching the case in point as expeditiously as possible, I soon made amends for my deprivation, by indulging in a little longer repose than usual, and on awaking I felt myself quite refreshed, and rather pleased than otherwise at finding myself thus suddenly at Mequinez; for having before passed the road more leisurely, and observed every thing worthy of remark, I did not so much regret that my journey had been performed during the night.

I have been four days here, and yesterday I was called upon to attend the captain of a band of huntsmen, who were that morning returned from an expedition, in which they lost three of their companions, and only succeeded in saving their chief, and bringing him to this place, by little short of a miracle. He has been lacerated in a most dreadful manner; his head is nearly scalped, and part of the integuments of his arms and back inverted. His condition is certainly dangerous; but, as he is a young and healthy subject, I do not despair of effecting his recovery.

I have learned the following particulars of this melancholy catastrophe. About fifty resolute young men marched hence, all armed and well stocked with ammunition and provisions, and accompanied by a mountaineer, who acted as guide. Their primary object was to destroy six young lions, that had committed terrible devastation in one of their villages; compelled the inhabitants to flee precipitately; and themselves remained sole masters of the *citadel*. After a march of three days, they arrived at the scene of action, and succeeded in destroying those lions; but hearing that there were more in the neighbourhood, they prepared to encounter them also. By order of this young man, who was chief of the company, they separated in five divisions, and repaired to different posts on the borders of the forest, to wait the arrival of the lions. They had not remained long, ere the terrific roar of these animals commenced, the sound approached nearer and nearer to their place of concealment, and one of the lions passed close to a party, and received the fire of their pieces; the animal darted upon them in return, before they could charge again, and three unfortunate men fell victims to his rage. The creature finding he had more enemies to contend with, and his wounds beginning to smart, retreated to a cover, where he sat licking them, and meditating another attack. He was on the point of springing on the captain, who had approached nearer to him than the rest, when the young man discharged his musket, the contents of which entered, and dislocated, the lower jaw of the enraged animal. The instant the youth had fired, he retreated with the utmost precipitation towards his companions, but his foot unfortunately slipping, he fell prostrate between two stones: in which position the lion assailed him; and being unable to tear him in pieces with his teeth, in consequence of the wound in his jaw, he made use of his tremendous paws, and would undoubtedly have destroyed him, but for the timely assistance of his comrades. The animal was so intent on the destruction of his enemy, that he received a close fire from two muskets, the muzzles of which nearly touched him. He no sooner found himself mortally wounded, than, raising the almost lifeless man in both paws, he dashed him on the ground, and fell dead by his side.

The man received a very severe contusion on his bead, which deprived him of sense for some time, and is what I dread the most in his case. His wounds were dressed by his companions in the best manner they could, and he was brought hither. The Emperor has very liberally rewarded him and his party, and made a handsome provision for the widows and children of those poor fellows who fell in the expedition. I sincerely hope this man may recover to enjoy the munificence of his Sovereign.

I have most excellent quarters here, contiguous to one of the palaces, and am allowed to walk or ride in the Imperial gardens, which are very extensive. The Emperor's palaces here, are much upon the same plan, with those at Fez, but larger. One of them is about three miles in circumference. All the apartments are on the ground floor, and are large long rooms, about twenty feet in height, receiving air from two folding doors which open into a square court, with a portico round, embellished with colonnades. The walls of the rooms are faced with glazed tiles, and the floors paved with the same, which gives an air of coolness and neatness, so desirable in this warm climate.

The seraglio of the Emperor, and indeed the harams of men of less rank, are sacred. No strangers are admitted, and it is profanation in a man to enter; but as a *tweeb*, I am privileged, and enjoy a liberty, never granted before. The day after my arrival, His Excellency the *Sheik* called upon me, and requested me to go home with him. He informed me that he had been assured, in the most positive manner, by all the doctors, and female attendants, that his wife had a dead child in her, and that nothing less than a miracle of their great Prophet could save her. The poor man was very much agitated while giving me this account. I find she is his favourite wife, and no wonder, for she is a very lovely woman. Upon examination, I found that what they imagined to be a dead child, is a protuberant hardness in the region of the liver, extending nearly all over the abdomen. The tumefaction was considered as a case of pregnancy; and she having considerably passed her time, the child was thought to be dead within her. I have begun a course of medicine, which I flatter myself will entirely eradicate the disorder.

My stay was so very short, when I was here before, that I could give you no account of the town, &c. The city of Mequinez is in the kingdom of Fez, and thirty miles from the capital of that name. The dynasty of *Mequinez* were the founders of this town, which they erected upon the ruins of the old one. Stephanus takes notice of it, by the name of *Gilda*, and says, that it was a place of great note. Marmol also asserts, that the present Mequinez answers in every respect to the ancient *Gilda*. It was considerably enlarged by Muley Ishmael, who (as well as several other Moorish princes, successively) defended himself in this place, against the attacks of the mountaineers. Several lines of circumvallation and intrenchments are still to be seen.

It is surrounded with walls, and fortified by two bastions; but has no artillery. It contains about one hundred thousand inhabitants; twenty-five thousand of whom are Jews, who have a town of their own, irregularly fortified, and guarded by a strong force, under the direction of an Alcaid, who is styled the Governor of the Jews.

There is not the smallest difference, in the construction of these houses, from those of Fez; though the inhabitants differ very materially. The men are of a short, thick, muscular make, and swarthy complexion, with long black beards and black eyes. The women are excessively handsome, and remarkably fair; nor are they devoid of neatness and elegance in their dress. They improve the beauty of their eyes with paint.

The Moorish inhabitants of this city are all militia-men, entirely at the disposal of the Emperor. They are excellent horsemen, expert at the sword and lance; and with fire-arms most admirable marksmen. They are generally considered barbarous and ferocious.

The people of distinction go about richly attired, having much gold and silver on their clothes. They take great pains in cleaning their teeth, combing their long beards, and keeping their nails pared extremely close.

The streets of this town are not paved; and the soil being clay, they must be very disagreeable in winter; for, after a heavy shower of rain, they are almost impassable from the accumulation of mud in every quarter. The market-places, with which this place abounds, are long, narrow, arched or covered streets, with small shops on each side, superintended by a Cadi, and an officer under him, for the purpose of collecting the duties on the sale of goods, &c. The chief furniture of the houses consists of beautiful carpets, cushions, and mattresses, upon which they sit and lie.

In and about the neighbourhood of this place are several saints' houses, near which no Christian, nor Jew, is allowed to pass. The most remarkable is the *hospitium* of Sidi-el-Marti.

The Emperor's favourite diversions, while here, are shooting and hunting, in both of which I am told he excels. He keeps a large pack of greyhounds, as fine as any I have seen in England. His pleasure-grounds, and park, in the vicinity of this town, abound in all kinds of game, hares, rabbits, and deer, and in wild boars and foxes.

LETTER XVI.

Courtship — Marriage — Funerals — Sabbath.

Mequinez.

I shall now give you an account of the manner in which the marriages are invariably negotiated and conducted in this country. A female, the confidential friend of the suitor, is dispatched to observe and report the beauty and accomplishments of the young lady; and when those are found to be perfectly adapted to the gentleman's taste, she is further delegated to sound his eulogium, and by every means, such as presenting her with valuable jewels, &c. to ingratiate him in the good opinion of the fair one. When this curious courtship ends, by terms being agreed upon, the destined bridegroom pays down a sum of money to the bride, a license is taken out from the Cadi, and the parties are married. I send you a description of a marriage-ceremony, at which I was present the other day.

The bridegroom (who is one of the officers of the household) came out of his house, attended by a vast number of his friends, and mounted one of the best horses belonging to the Emperor, most curiously and richly caparisoned. He carried his sword unsheathed, and was preceded by a splendid standard, and a band of music; he was followed by a kind of palanquin, supported on the shoulders of four stout black slaves, a detachment of cavalry firing off their pieces every minute, and a procession of relatives and friends, the whole moving with great mirth and jollity,

Before they reached the house of the bride, the cavalcade halted, and the bridegroom dismounted, assisted by his negro slaves, and knocked loudly at the door three times. The lady was brought out in a covered chair, attended by four women, completely muffled up. The whole party of the bridegroom turned their backs, and she was smuggled into the palanquin: they then returned in the same style to the house of her lord, where, before she was allowed to enter, he placed himself at the entrance, and extending his right arm across the door-way, she passed under, as an indication of her voluntary and unconditional submission to his will and pleasure.

After this ceremony, the bridegroom was obliged to retire to the house of his nearest relation, where he continued three days and nights, feasting, and receiving presents from all his male friends, while the bride was paid the same compliments by her female acquaintance. At the expiration of the appointed time, the gentleman returned to his own house.

The Moors are not allowed by their law more than four wives, but they may have as many concubines as they can maintain; accordingly, the wealthy Moors, besides their wives, keep a kind of seraglio of women of all colours.

From their marriages, I am insensibly led to the subject of the burial of their dead. Not that any idea strikes me of an analogy between the situations of a married person, and one consigned to the *"narrow house,"* as Ossian poetically styles the grave; but from a certain succession of thought, for which one is at a loss to account. In the burial of their dead, they are decent and pious, without pomp or show. The corpse is attended by the relations and friends, chanting passages from the Koran, to the mosque, where it is washed, and it is afterwards interred in a place at some distance from the town, the Iman, or priest, pronouncing an oration, containing the eulogy of the deceased. The male relations express their regard by alms and prayers, the women by ornamenting the tomb with flowers and green leaves. Their term of mourning is the same as ours, twelve months, during which period the widows divest themselves of every ornament, and appear habited in the coarsest attire. Their burial-grounds are inclosed by cypress and other dark lofty trees, the lower parts of which are interwoven with odoriferous shrubs and creeping plants, forming an almost impenetrable hedge. Some of their tombs are very curious, though they exhibit specimens of the rudest architecture. There are also several saints' houses in their burying-places, which render them doubly sacred; and no Christian or Jew is suffered to enter, on pain of death.

Friday being their Sabbath, the day is kept perfectly holy; all the Moors are employed in prayer, reading the Koran, or visiting the tombs of their departed friends.

Curiosity prompted me to go and see an assemblage of fanatics, at a celebrated saint's house, in the neighbourhood of this town. They were to perform many wonderful things, such as tearing a live sheep in pieces, and devouring the flesh, fighting with wild beasts, and several other barbarous exhibitions. These people, called in Barbary *Free Masons*, are nothing more than a set of canting, roaring companions, surcharged with wine and other liquors, and assembled in this holy place, for the sole purpose of giving free vent to their brutal passions. This society is peculiar to itself, having no connexion with our ancient or modern Free Masons. I have however obtained a free access to their saints' houses and secret meetings, with permission to go any where unmolested; but I always take the precaution to go well armed, and escorted by the Emperor's guards, as nothing can exceed the barbarous acts of this fanatic set of people.

I am extremely happy to say, that my most sanguine expectations with regard to the poor man, whose accident I mentioned in my last, are realized; every unfavourable symptom has vanished, and I can safely rely on his perfect recovery. The complaint of my female patient has also given way to a proper course of medicine, and the Governor is one of the happiest of men. When I announced the pleasing intelligence of her disease being removed, he embraced me with such ecstacy that I almost dreaded suffocation; in short, he has spared nothing that can evince his gratitude and satisfaction, for what he terms the inestimable benefit I have conferred upon him.

The country round this city is inexpressibly rich and beautiful, being laid put for several miles in gardens, abounding in flowers and fruit-trees; among the latter the vine sands pre-eminent, yielding most delicious grapes. The air here, as in the other parts of Barbary, is very pure and salubrious.

LETTER XVII.

Depart for Morocco — Roads dreadfully infested, by Robbers — A Tribe of aboriginal Freebooters — Description of Morocco — Filth of the common People — Tobacco disallowed — Justice of the Emperor.

Mequinez

Since I wrote last, I have taken a trip to Morocco and back again. As I had a great deal of leisure time, and every thing here having lost the attraction of novelty, I determined to go further up the interior of the country; and accordingly applied to the Emperor for permission to visit Morocco, which he granted, but with the injunction that I should return as quickly as possible.

I set off, accompanied by my usual guard, which I assure you I never found so necessary as on this journey; for the rapacious spirit of the peasantry exposed us continually to the danger of being plundered, we were therefore obliged to keep watch alternately, to prevent our property, perhaps our lives, becoming a prey to these wretches. The neighbourhood of Morocco is dreadfully infested by robbers and assassins.

The inhabitants of the empire of Morocco, that are not in a military capacity, or otherwise immediately in the service of the Emperor, are miserably poor; and the natural indolence of their disposition preventing them from making any laudable exertions towards gaining a livelihood, they have recourse to every means of fraud and violence. It is astonishing how frequently assassinations and robberies are committed in this empire, notwithstanding the ruffians, when detected, are punished in the most exemplary manner, by the right hand and left foot being cut off, and the head afterwards being severed from the body. The relations of the murderer are all fined very heavily, and the judgment often extends to the whole village, near which the crime had been perpetrated; yet seldom a day passes but some daring robbery is committed, accompanied by the most wanton and savage cruelty; the unhappy victim of the plunderer being frequently left in the public roads in a most shocking state of mutilation.

Another ostensible cause of the dereliction of the peasantry from the laws of humanity, may be the extreme oppression under which they groan; as, on account of their former propensity to rebellion, they are now ruled with a rod of iron, which in all probability has rendered them callous, and deaf to the voice of nature. But, independently of these occasional depredations, there is a band of vagrants, who are actuated by no other motives, than what their own black hearts suggest. They inhabit caves in the sides of enormous rocky precipices, and go entirely naked: their principal food is the flesh of wild beasts. This tribe of freebooters appears to be quite a distinct set of people; they seem to have an invincible aversion to the Mahometan religion, and worship the *sun* and *fire*; they speak a different language from the rest of the inhabitants, a mixture of African and the *old* Arabic; all which circumstances favour their own report of themselves, which is, that they are the genuine descendants of the original inhabitants. They look down upon the more civilized Moors with contempt, and consider them as the real usurpers of their country, and the plunderers of their property. They subsist chiefly by rapine, and frequently throw a whole village into consternation by their nocturnal visits; yet their cunning and dexterity are so great, that they almost constantly elude the vigilance of justice: indeed, they are never forced from their places of retreat (which are inaccessible to all but themselves), but when taken, it is either in the act of robbing, or when they venture to the markets or fairs; and then the capture is not effected without a strong body of the military.

I was much disappointed on my arrival at Morocco with the appearance of the place; for, instead of finding it, as I expected, superior to Fez and Mequinez, I found it a large ruinous town, almost without inhabitants. It contains, indeed, a great many mosques, caravanseras, public baths, marketplaces or squares, and palaces of the Xeriffes, but all in almost deplorable state of ruin. Not many years since, this city was the Imperial residence, and contained six hundred and fifty thousand inhabitants; but the late civil wars, and the plague, which raged with such violence, in the beginning of the present Emperor's reign, nearly depopulated it. In consequence of the latter melancholy event, the court was removed to Fez and Mequinez. To this account we may place the present desolate appearance of Morocco. The Imperial palace is, however, kept in repair, as the Emperor goes to Morocco annually to spend the fast-days, which are during the months of October and November; scarcely one fourth of the other palaces and houses are inhabited; but though this city now exhibits evident symptoms of rapid decay, we may still form a just idea of its former grandeur and magnificence.

The plain of Morocco is bounded by that long ridge of mountains called *Atlas*, which screen the town from the scorching heat of the easterly winds, while the snow, with which their summits are covered, renders the climate more temperate than in other parts of Barbary. Notwithstanding the salubrity of the climate of Morocco, a residence there is rendered miserable, by the multitudes of scorpions, serpents, gnats, and bugs, which infest the town and its neighbourhood.

His Imperial Majesty holds a court of justice here, previous to the commencement of the holidays, and also issues orders for a general ablution by men, women, and children, of every class: this, no doubt, is very necessary, as the common people seldom change their linen, and the greater part of them are covered with vermin. During the fast they dare not touch any food while the sun is up, and when at night they are allowed to break their fast, they absolutely make perfect beasts of themselves. Smoking, or chewing tobacco, and taking snuff, are strictly prohibited, by an edict from the Emperor: the vender is punished with the bastinado, and a confiscation of all his goods and cattle, and the buyer with six years imprisonment.

Owing to the intense heat of the weather lately, there is a great scarcity of water: so that we were obliged to carry it up in bags made of goat-skin, to supply us on the road; and coming back we took the same precaution.

When at Morocco, I was extremely anxious to visit *Mogedor*, a sea-port town, and the island of *Erythia*, now also called Mogedor, which island contains a castle of considerable strength, defended by a strong garrison, stationed there chiefly, as I have been told, to protect the gold-mines in the neighbourhood; but the distance was very great, and my time so limited, that I could not spare a fortnight, which it would at least have required to get there and back again. I have been returned here two days, and, as I observed before, not so much gratified as I expected.

As I passed one of the courts of the palace yesterday, a fellow was receiving punishment for a robbery. The right hand and foot were severed at the articulation, by a single blow of a large axe; the stumps were immediately immersed in a vessel of boiling pitch; and in this miserable condition he was turned about his business. I once attended a man who had suffered these amputations; he soon recovered, and, to my great surprise, instead of sorrowing for his loss, he skipped about as nimbly as possible, and afterwards enlisted in the police. After the fellow was turned away yesterday, a peasant, who had walked nearly two hundred miles, presented himself before the Emperor, to complain of the Governor of his province, for not having done him justice in assisting him to recover a debt of about six shillings. The Emperor listened to his grievance, issued an order to enforce the payment of the debt, and gave the poor man a sum of money to enable him to return home.

LETTER XVIII.

Moorish Character — Form of Devotion — Meals — Revenue — Poll-tax on the Jews — Royal Carriages — Ostrich-riding — Public Schools — Watch-dogs.

Mequinez.

The established religion of the Moors is Mahometan. Formerly, as well as at present, women were considered by the Moors as the mere objects of sensuality, and only esteemed while in full bloom. At the age of thirty, or at most forty, they were looked upon as an inferior order of beings, and doomed to the most abject and insupportable slavery: indeed, the latter circumstance still exists, though considerably mitigated. No wonder then that the doctrine of Mahomet should be cordially embraced by a people with whose inclinations it so exactly coincided. But that part only was adopted, which indulged them in the gratification of their wishes; that which imposed restraint was renounced, or only nominally acceded to. And fortunate it certainly is for the security of the neighbouring countries that they did so; as, when formerly they were inured from infancy to all the hardships of a warlike life, and possessed much skill in war, they were undoubtedly very formidable; but since their conversion to Mahometanism, they have gradually become inactive, and their natural passion for war and conquest has changed to absolute effeminacy. The illiterate system of the Moors has also completely shut the door against the arts and sciences, and all knowledge of the value of a free and secure commerce. Yet, notwithstanding this people are no longer either in appearance or reality those fierce barbarians they once were, nor can their actions in point of valour bear any comparison with those of their ancestors, like them they retain a most inveterate antipathy to all Christians; and a propensity towards cruelty, revenge, rapine, and murder, still continues to form one of the most prominent features of their character. However, under the comparatively mild government of the present Emperor, their behaviour towards Christians has visibly undergone a favourable change, which would almost persuade some to indulge a hope of the entire annihilation of their aversion; but I am sorry to add, that I am not so sanguine, as from accurate observation I have been led to conclude, that nothing but an immense length of time can overcome their habitual prejudices and constitutional inclinations.

The male inhabitants of these states are obliged to attend their places of public worship four times in the course of twenty-four hours. The first prayer begins about half an hour before sun-rising, and is so regulated that they may, just as the sun rises, finish eight adorations. They pray again at noon, at sun-set, and at midnight: they are very fervent in their devotions, and always turn their faces towards the east: they fast three times in a year; the first time thirty days, the next nine, and the last seven: during these fasts they abstain from beans, garlic, and some other pulse and vegetables. They call the Almighty, *God of Gods*, and *Lord of Lords*; and they all believe that the souls of wicked men will be punished till a certain period, when they will be received to mercy.

In the morning, after prayer, they drink strong tea, which they prefer to coffee. At eleven o'clock they, go to dinner, which consists of fruits, sweetmeats, and their favourite *cous-ca-sou*, piled up in a large wooden bowl. Their chief meal is after their return from evening prayer. They eat cakes made of fine wheaten flour; and as they consider it a crime to cut bread or meat of any kind after it is dressed, these cakes are made so thin that they may be easily broken with the hands; and their meat, which is generally mutton or fowls, is so prepared that they can without difficulty separate it from the bones with their fingers. They sit cross-legged upon cushions, and devour their food very greedily and without the least ceremony. Although sobriety is strictly enjoined by the Mahometan law, yet the Moorish inhabitants of the principal towns in Barbary make free with most excellent wines and spirits of their own manufacture.

The revenues of the Emperor have of late augmented prodigiously. He receives a tenth part of all the property of his Mahometan subjects; and he compels every Jew residing in his dominions to pay a poll-tax of six crowns annually. The number of Israelites subject to the Emperor of Morocco exceeds one hundred thousand. They are strictly guarded, and cruelly oppressed, and are not permitted to quit the states without a special leave from the Emperor, to obtain which they are obliged to pay down a large sum of money.

The authority of the Emperor is unlimited, as is that of his Governors, who possess a power of life and death. No rank nor condition of Moors is exempt from taxation, excepting the immediate princes of the blood, and the *Xeriffes*, which are the only degrees of nobility the Moors have. The Xeriffes are the descendants of their monarchs, and their titles are hereditary: but the title of *Sheik* is temporary; so that the respect paid to the Sheiks on account of their high situations expires with them.

Coaches, carriages, and palanquins are used only by the Emperor. I have seen some, both here and at Fez, which are really elegant; they are for the use of his ladies when they go to spend the day in any of the Imperial gardens. The Emperor has several very handsome chariots, in one of which he usually rides, drawn by six mules. The Moors ride on horseback, attended by a number of slaves or soldiers, according to their rank and wealth.

The princes of the blood and Xeriffes are not allowed to interfere in any political or public business, and are never consulted in state affairs. They are generally provided for, with sinecure places to support their rank, but many of these are too small to enable them to do so. The several Governors of provinces have each a large tract of land; and the tax collected from the venders and buyers in the weekly markets in their districts is also appropriated by them to defray the charges of their retinue and troops. From the vast crown lands in this country, the Emperor obtains sufficient for the expenses of the court, household, and great officers of state; from which circumstance, and what I have before said of his revenues, it is evident that his coffers must be most abundantly supplied, and his annual saving in ordinary cases very great. A detachment of troops from each province is sent every three months to collect the tributes, which are levied with the most unrelenting rigour. There are some vestiges of the Caliphate government still remaining; for in places where no military officer resides, the Mufti, or high-priest, is the fountain of all justice; he collects the tributes, and under him the Cadis or civil officers act in the same manner as our justices of the peace.

The general language of the country is Arabic; but in the inland countries, in the provinces of Suz, Tafilet, and Gessula, the ancient African language is still spoken. Those remote districts are now under the sovereignty of the Emperor of Morocco; but I am told they contain nothing particularly curious, except an immense number of pelicans and ostriches, the latter so strong as to be able to carry a man upon their backs. I one day saw a Moor riding in a court here upon one, which he had got from those parts, and tamed for. show.

The Moors write in the manner of the Hebrew language, from right to left; they are wonderfully expeditious in it, and their seals are very neat. Public schools have lately been established in all the towns and villages of these states; but, as the children are taught by their priests, a set of superstitious and fanatic people, no great benefit, to change or improve their manners, can accrue from such an institution.

I believe, in a former letter I told you that the peasantry reside in tents; I have however observed a few huts built of clay, but very few. In the centre of both the huts and tents, there is a hole dug in the ground, where they make a fire, with an outlet in the roof to vent the smoke. They generally burn wood, or a species of charcoal, in the preparation of which they contrive to deprive it of the baneful effects usually experienced from the use of it in England. They have mats spread round the fire, upon which they sit in the day, and sleep at night. They are so parsimonious, that they live the greater part of the year on fruit, vegetables, and fish, though they supply the markets with abundance of fowls (of which they rear immense numbers), butter, &c. &c. Their chief defence at night is their dogs; each tent is provided with one, and they are so vigilant, that they give instant notice of the approach of intruders; and when the alarm is communicated to the whole of them, it is scarcely possible to conceive the effect. The habit of the peasantry is the same both winter and summer, and consists of a thick garment (frequently old and tattered), a short capote, a greasy turban, and a pair of yellow slippers. They sometimes throw round them a coarse white *haik*, which also serves for a bed and covering in the night, as many of them lie upon the bare ground in the open air before their tents.

In my next I shall give you a short sketch of the produce of this fertile country.

LETTER XIX.

Face and Produce of the Empire, natural and artificial.

Mequinez.

The mountains (the principal of which are Mount Diur, Mount Cotta, near the city of Larache, the mountain commonly called *Ape's Hill*, between Tangiers and Ceuta, and that remarkable ridge called Mount Atlas) contain mines of gold, silver, copper, and tin.

The chief capes or promontories of these states are, Cape Cottes or Ampelusia, known to our seafaring people by the name of Cape Spartel, the *Promontorium Herculis*, and the *Promontorium Oleastrum*, so called from the prodigious number of wild olives growing upon it.

All the bays round the coast furnish an abundance of the most delicious fish of every kind; and the several rivers are equally productive. The occasional overflow of the rivers greatly enriches and fertilizes the soil, to which, more than to their own industry (for they never manure their grounds, and are absolute strangers to the art of husbandry), are the Moors indebted for their plentiful crops of wheat, Turkey corn, rye, rice, oats, barley, and grain of all kinds.

I have before told you that this country abounds in fine fruits. The most esteemed are, oranges, grapes, pomegranates, lemons, citrons, figs, almonds, and dates. The Moors also grow great quantities of excellent hemp and flax. Medicinal herbs and roots are very plentiful here. Vegetables of every kind, and melons, cucumbers, &c. thrive exceedingly well. The grass grows spontaneously to an amazing height, and in consequence of the fine pasturage the animals are very prolific, cows and mares producing two at a birth, and the sheep frequently four lambs in the year.

Among the botanical herbs, plants, and roots, are the colocynth, palma Christi, wild and meadow saffron, the great mountain garlic, mountain satyrion, senna, rhubarb, bastard rhubarb, balsam apple, horned poppy, wild succory, recabilia peruviana, ipecacuanha, wild turnip, wild radish, field mustard, Indian cress, dandelion, black winter cherry, wild lily, hyacinth, violet, narcissus, wild rose, camomile, tulips, and the *fleur de lis*, equal to that of Florence; with a variety of others too numerous to describe.

The domestic animals of these states are, the horse, ass, mule, rumrah (a beast of burden in the mountainous parts), camel, dromedary, antelope, cow, dog, sheep, and large goat. The beasts of prey are, lions, tigers, leopards, hyenas, and wolves. The apes are innumerable. Deer, wild boars, hares, rabbits, ferrets, weazels, moles, and camelions, are also found in great numbers. Horses and cattle of all kinds are sold at very low prices.

Among the feathered tribe most common here, are, very large eagles, hawks, partridges, quails, wild pigeons, and wild fowl of every kind, turtle-doves, and a variety of small birds; among which the capsa sparrow is remarkable for the elegance of its plumage and the sweetness of its notes, in which it excels every other bird: this beautiful little creature cannot live out of its native country. I had almost forgotten to mention the storks and cranes, which are seen here in great numbers, and so extremely tame, from being perfectly unmolested, that they build their nests and rear their young in the very centre of the towns and villages, and on the tops of the towers of their mosques. Of the reptile kind, venomous spiders, scorpions, vipers, and enormously large serpents, are common in Barbary.

The greatest natural curiosities of this country are the salt-pits (which in some places are immensely large), and several hot springs, possessing such a great degree of heat, that an egg being put in for a short time will become quite hard. The face of the country itself is a natural curiosity; the vallies, which are several leagues in extent, and the mountains, which reach as far as the deserts of Suz, Tafilet, and Gessula, interspersed with forests or corn-fields, and rich meadows, are remarkably curious.

The artificial curiosities are very numerous, and claim the attention of all who may visit this country. They ought properly to be divided into two classes; in the first of which may be placed the subterraneous cavern and passage near Tangiers; the ruins of the amphitheatres, triumphal arches, temples, &c. erected by the Carthaginians, Romans, and Arabs, at Fez and the several other towns of Barbary. The country is besides all over scattered with the remains of ditches and ramparts, evidently designed for the defence of camps, forts, and castles, no other vestiges of which, however, can be found. Besides these, I have observed a number of round towers, which appear to have belonged, some to houses of religion, and others to the palaces or residences of former rulers in this country.

In the second class, we may place the efforts of the architectural and mechanical genius of the present inhabitants, exemplified in the wonderful aqueducts at Morocco, which commence in Mount Atlas (by the natives called *Gibbel-el-Hadith*), and convey water in the greatest abundance to all the houses of the city and its environs. Nor is the wheel at Fez, which I mentioned in a former letter, less worthy of remark; and several mausoleums in their burial-places have been constructed in a very costly style, the stucco of the walls being remarkably smooth and beautiful, and as hard as marble; but these tombs are exceptions to the general rule; for, as I have before observed, the greater part are but rude buildings. There are many other curiosities, which to describe minutely would fill a volume.

LETTER XX.

Practice of Physic – Astrology – Poetry – Entertainment given by the Author to the Moors – Their Astonishment at the Effects of Electricity.

Mequinez.

I shall now speak of their principal or rather only studies, which are, physic, astrology, and poetry. First then of physic, to give you an accurate idea of the extent of their knowledge in which, it will be sufficient to describe their practice of it; and I am sure you, my dear D――, and every other friend to humanity, will agree with me, that it would have been better for their countrymen if they had never attempted it at all, as unassisted nature would do more, for those afflicted with disease, than such bunglers.

The general practice adopted by the Moorish physicians, or *Tweebs*, is, bleeding *ad deliquium* in all fevers; administering excessive doses of drastic medicines, plenty of emulsions, and a watery diet. They order vinegar in cases of quinsies and ardent fevers, and garlic in those of a putrid, malignant, and pestilential kind. They prescribe alum in cases of hemorrhage and dysentery; hot spices and long abstinences in chronic diseases; recent ox-gall to kill worms and cure dropsies; castor and myrrh in all hysteric affections; asses milk in slow fevers and consumptions; oranges, honey, eggs, mint, and myrrh, in cases of typhus; poppy-juice in convulsive disorders and fluxes of the bowels; pitch or tar water and pennyroyal in common fevers; rose-leaves in cases of diabetes; and sulphur in all cutaneous disorders. This is the whole of the Moorish *materia medica*. In simple diseases, where little medical ability is necessary, and the good habit of body of these people in general contributes to their success, they may effect a cure; but in desperate cases, where nothing but the skill of the physician can relieve oppressed nature, it is not astonishing that they should fail. These men are in some measure astrologers: most probably, being gifted with a greater degree of cunning than their neighbours, they have discovered the weak side of their countrymen, together with their own insufficiency, to cover which they pretend to a knowledge of the stars, which has the greatest weight with the superstitious Moors; consequently, when a patient, either by their improper treatment, or the violence of his disease, evinces symptoms of approaching dissolution, the doctor, with infinite gravity, points out to the surrounding relations the star which, he positively asserts, appears to summon the dying man to the bosom of his Prophet. By this means he avoids reproach, since he has made it so evident, that the poor man's time was come, and that nothing could ward off the shafts of destiny. This apparently wonderful faculty of prognostication, added to their exemplary mode of living, and liberal donations to the poor and afflicted, operating upon the minds of the blind and fanatic Moors, induces *them* to consider their physicians next to their saints, and to worship *them* with nearly as much reverence.

The Tweebs have each from two to six disciples, whom they instruct and initiate in their secrets of the healing art. In their regular visits to any town, they parade the streets with great pomp and gravity, followed by a train of miserable objects, who pretend to have been recently recovered from a long and dangerous illness by the extraordinary skill of the doctor; while, in fact, their cadaverous countenances and emaciated bodies seem to contradict their assertions, and bear ample testimony that they are hurrying fast to that country, "from whose bourne no traveller returns." Under the pretence of charity, these poor wretches are supported by this Moorish AEsculapius, while his views in so doing are entirely selfish; that by their means he may better impose on the credulous, and obtain considerable sums of money. When any one of them (by chance) effects what he considers a great cure, it is communicated in a circular letter to all the doctors in Barbary.

They select one of their elders every year, and appoint him to preside over them. His business, for the time being, is to settle all their controversies: he is the fountain of all justice among them; for as they are looked upon to be petty saints, they are a privileged set of men, and not in the least subject to either civil or military jurisdiction. They possess the art of taming the monstrous serpents of the country, and rendering them perfectly harmless: in short, their profession is nothing but a system of the grossest empiricism.

Formerly the country could boast of having scientific astronomers; for, like the ancient Egyptians, the inhabitants of Barbary cultivated the science of astronomy with great success; but as it was communicated from generation to generation by tradition only, it is not surprising that the increasing indolence of the Moors should have made them relinquish the more abstruse parts, and that now it is dwindled into mere astrology. Their habitual mode of living, frequently exposed at night, during all weathers, in the open air, enables them without difficulty to observe the fixed stars, and their influence on the weather, and they have thence ascribed to every one some peculiar property, by which the events of human life, good or bad, are regulated.

In poetry I am told the Moors are very successful. The subjects of their poems are mostly eulogies of the great men who have belonged to the tribe of which the poet is a member: these compositions are all extempore, like those of our ancient bards, or those of the Celts, spoken of by Julius Cæsar, who wandered about in Gaul and other parts of the continent with their harps. The poets of Barbary have no settled home, but with an instrument somewhat resembling a mandolin they wander from place to place, and house to house, composing and singing pieces improviso, on the honour and antiquity of their tribe. From persons acquainted with the language, I have heard, that they are very happy in this species of poetry, which is far from deficient in point of harmony. For myself I can say, that though unable to enter into the spirit of it from the circumstance of not perfectly understanding the language, yet I was much pleased with the effect.

I shall conclude this letter with a short description of an entertainment which I gave to several of the inhabitants of this place a few days since. Having invited as many as I could conveniently accommodate, I regaled them with all the most exquisite things the market afforded. I passed the bottle pretty briskly, telling them the liquor was a favourite decoction of mine, which they might drink without any scruple. They did not seem to wish to doubt this assertion; and having raised their spirits to a flow of mirth and jollity, I told them, that, as they had done me the honour of coming to dine with me, I would endeavour to amuse them with a small specimen of what the doctors in England commonly make use of in certain chronical complaints. I then placed my electric machine in the centre of the court, and having loaded it with a sufficient quantity of electric fluid, produced such a powerful shock to about a dozen of the stoutest, that, either from surprise or terror, they fell apparently senseless on the floor. The consternation and confusion which ensued were beyond description; the rest were all retiring precipitately with the most dreadful yells and cries imaginable, expecting to share the fate of their companions. With much difficulty I prevailed on them to remain, and, raising the men from the ground, I convinced them they had received no injury; upon which they unanimously attributed it to my great skill in magic, and loaded me with a thousand compliments, I repeated the experiment three or four times, to their inexpressible wonder, and I was at length almost hailed as a supernatural being. The report of this extraordinary phenomenon soon spread abroad, and a vast concourse of people assembled; but my guard would not allow any one to enter without my permission. In the evening I sent for a band of music, and my company continued dancing and rioting till morning. They brought in several Jewish women, and carried the farce to such a length, that I was completely rejoiced to get rid of them, determining, in my own mind, never again to venture such another entertainment.

LETTER XXI.

Prevalent Diseases – Abuse of Stimulants – Medicinal Well – Sorcery – Hydrophobia.

Mequinez.

Although the plague is not so common in these states as in Turkey and Egypt, yet it is often brought hither by means of the caravans, and several articles of luxury imported annually by the merchants from Mecca and Medina; and, for want of proper precaution, it is suffered to spread, to desolate, and to stop of its own accord; for the Moors continue obstinately blinded by the same superstitious and absurd notions that are entertained by the Mahometans of the Turkish empire, of its being a punishment occasionally inflicted upon the true believers by their angry Prophet, and that it is incurable; and here I receive on this subject the same tales and romantic accounts that I did during my residence in Egypt in the year 1801.

The most prevailing diseases in this country that have come under my observation, are, cutaneous disorders of all kinds, intermittent fevers, those of a putrid, malignant, pestilential kind, and the puerperal fever, which proceeds from the barbarous treatment of lying-in women in this country, as they are kept in small confined rooms, deprived of the benefit of pure air.

One day I went to see a very fine young woman, the lady of one of the Xeriffes. The heat of the room was intolerable. After much persuasion, I succeeded in having her removed to a cooler one, and she recovered, contrary to the predictions of the female attendant, who reported the daily changes to a celebrated doctor here. It is wonderful what numbers of young women fall victims to this fever in the course of a year.

Besides the above-mentioned complaints, I have observed insanity, epilepsy, spasmodic affections of the face, ruptures of all kinds (which last are produced by their loose kind of trowsers); nervous consumptions, extreme debility, and dropsy, brought on by their indolent manner of living, and the great abuses of violent doses of drastic medicines.

The principal and opulent inhabitants of this country, in order to excite certain desires, are frequently in the habit of receiving, from their own doctors, several strong and powerful stimulants, to the infallible detriment and ultimate, destruction of their constitutions. I have been at great pains to deter them from these abominable habits, by representing to them their ill effects and fatal consequences; but as they all appear to have a great propensity for a short life and a merry one, I fear my advice has been thrown away, for I have daily the most pressing and importunate solicitations from all classes of people, both young and old, to give them the medicines I have alluded to:—but 1 must here be clearly understood, that debauchery which exists in all the principal towns of this country in a superlative degree, does not extend to the inland and mountainous parts, where the morals are pure, and the people remarkably healthy, strong, and robust, living to a very advanced age, and scarcely ever afflicted with any disease excepting cutaneous disorders, to which they are very subject. The great abuse of blood-letting on all trifling occasions, practised by the rich inhabitants, produces very bad effects.

There is a well in the neighbourhood of this town, which possesses a great many medicinal virtues; and though I have not been able to ascertain its mineral qualities, I have found, by using the water, that it is extremely friendly to the stomach, that it excites appetite and digestion, and lively spirits; that it is efficacious in the cure of gravel and nephritic complaints; and in cases of foulness of the blood, I have found it superior to any mineral waters I have met with in Europe. It has completely cured my Jew servant of a most inveterate scurvy, under which he had laboured for a very considerable time.

Notwithstanding the Moors possess this inestimable treasure near one of their most opulent and populous cities, yet, owing to fabulous tales, handed down by tradition from one generation to another, these superstitious people will never drink or disturb the water; to do so is reckoned sacrilege, and the offender is severely punished: for they positively affirm, that one of their great saints has been transmuted into it, and that at some distant period he will resume his natural form, to perform a great many miracles, and to render the Moors rich and happy, more so indeed than Mahomet has promised them in the other world.

While I have been here, I have had daily intercourse with the most eminent of their Tweebs. They pay me regular morning visits, questioning me on several points. One day I was asked by what means health was preserved, and what produced disease in the human body; I answered, that, "among several other remote causes, the air, by its different constitutions, had a great effect upon the human frame: that diseases revolve periodically, and keep time and measure exactly with the seasons of the year; and that either health or disease depended in some measure on the universal influence of the air, by its gravity, heat, cold, moisture, dryness, or exhalations." They have no idea of natural philosophy, nor of the knowledge and physiology of the air, or how to change and destroy its bad qualities in close and confined places. After much persuasion, I prevailed on some of them to make use of the fuming mixture of brimstone and aromatic ingredients, in all cases of pestilential fevers. Though this is not so efficacious as the nitrous acid, yet it will considerably abate the progress of contagion, and they are acquainted with the materials of the former, whereas they have not the smallest idea of the latter.

They are perfectly ignorant of the animal and comparative anatomy, and of physiology and pathology. They have no notion either of the nervous fluid, or of the solids, their restriction and relaxation. They have no other idea of the fluids than the blood, to a superabundance of which they attribute all the diseases incident to the human body. In the spring they recommend bleeding, to ensure a good state of health for the remainder of the year. These Tweebs are wonderfully reserved in all their actions.

The Moors have great faith in sorcery and witchcraft. I was called upon to visit a young man about eighteen, who was universally believed to be possessed by an evil spirit. His case was a confirmed hydrophobia. I informed the people that the disease was occasioned by the bite of a mad dog, and that the man would die in the course of the ensuing night. I inquired the next morning, when I found that I had judged correctly. I have also visited several young women who were reported to have been bewitched. Some I found labouring under the last stage of a nervous consumption; others under a dangerous and incurable lunacy. In short, nothing can exceed the ignorance and superstition of these deluded people.

I am afraid, my dear D— —, I have trespassed on your patience, both in this letter and the last, as nothing but physic and its practitioners have been introduced and discussed. I have certainly been too selfish; for, while I have been pursuing a subject the most interesting to me from the nature of my profession, a thought never once obtruded itself, that my friend perhaps would take no interest in the relation. However, by way of compensation, I give you leave to wish the Moorish physicians and their physic at the bottom of the Red Sea, and me with them, if you choose; but I have now done with them, and my next will, most probably, not be from Mequinez, as I think I have a good opportunity of returning to Gibraltar.

LETTER XXII.

Depart for Gibraltar – Oppressive Heat – Robbers – Arrive at Larache – Affray of some English Sailors – Letter from the Governor to Lord Collingwood.

Larache, August I, 1806.

I was perfectly right in my conjectures, that you would hear no more from me at Mequinez. Having succeeded in curing the patients under my care, and no disease of any consequence prevailing in the country, I thought it a favourable opportunity to request permission of the Emperor to return to Gibraltar; and having obtained it, I set off for this place.

On my way hither, I experienced the most dreadful inconvenience from the heat of the weather; it was oppressive in the extreme, and I was constantly annoyed with the sight of dead horses, mules, asses, cows, &c. that had perished on the road, from excessive heat and want of water. The rivers which I had observed on my way to Mequinez, and the waters of which I had so much relished, I now found completely dried up. We also suffered considerably from the want of fresh water, for that we had brought with us in bags became so hot, that nothing but the most dire necessity could have compelled us to make use of it; fortunately we now and then met with fields full of fine water-melons, of a most exquisite flavour: we sought them with the greatest avidity, and obtained relief from the excessive thirst with which we were oppressed. We were obliged to make very short stages, and to halt every hour under the shade of some tall trees, to recover ourselves.

I have had two or three most unpleasant encounters (on my way from Mequinez) with robbers. In the first I ran the risk of my life. It was the sixth day after we left Mequinez, as I was loitering considerably in the rear of my party, I was accosted by a common Moor on horseback, who, after surveying me from head to foot, asked for a pinch of snuff, which I gave him; then spying the gold chain of my watch, he attempted to seize it; but I prevented him by spurring my horse and galloping off to join my guard: the fellow fired his piece, which fortunately missed, and gave me an opportunity of returning the compliment, and of wounding him; when perceiving my guard coming at full speed to my assistance, wounded as he was, he made off across the fields, and was soon out of sight. This event (which, had I been in other circumstances, would have had no weight with me) I frankly confess so much agitated my spirits, already exhausted by the intense heat and intolerable thirst under which I suffered, that I found myself unable to proceed much further. At a little distance was a forest, and to the shade of that we determined to repair for the rest of the day, provided we could find a convenient spot to pitch our tents upon. We reached it about nine o'clock in the morning: I was assisted to dismount, and stretching myself on the burnt grass, under a clump of olive-trees, I desired my men to look about for a place to erect our tents. After a few minutes absence, they returned with the joyful intelligence, that they had met with a fine spring of water, and near it a sufficient space for our tents. This might indeed be called resuscitation to our drooping spirits. I arose with more alertness than I thought possible, and followed my men to this delightful spot. My wine was expended, and we were therefore glad of a glass of spirits and water, which completely recovered us; and we were enabled to enjoy a good dinner, which my Jew servant prepared.

We encamped, on this spot, for the night also; and from the occurrence of the morning, I thought it highly expedient to take every measure to prevent a repetition. I therefore ordered two or three fires to be kindled round our tents, and placed several sentinels about, to watch if any one approached. Having made these arrangements, and given strict orders to the serjeant to be on the alert, I repaired to rest; but there certainly was some spell, to prevent my enjoying what I stood so much in need of, a *sound* sleep. I had retired, but a very short time, to my tent, when I was suddenly roused by an alarm of The robbers! the robbers! The ruffians had contrived to slip in so privately, that, unperceived, they carried off one of my trunks, and were in the act of mounting two of my mules, when they were detected. They instantly made off with the trunk and mules. The confusion among my people was much greater than was necessary, and some time was lost in useless upbraidings.

I went out with the intention of calling the serjeant to a severe account, when I was informed that he had just gone in pursuit with six others. Those that remained kept vigilant watch with me the rest of the night. At break of day our party returned. They soon came up with the robbers, who, finding themselves so closely pursued, and likely to be overtaken, relinquished their booty to facilitate their escape. I had the satisfaction therefore to recover my trunk and mules. The serjeant employed the whole of his rhetorical abilities to give weight to the affair. I soon perceived that his account was much exaggerated, and immediately comprehended that his drift was to obtain a reward from me. I did not disappoint him, but ordered an extra allowance of rum to him and the rest of the party. As you may suppose, I was very anxious to quit a place where I had been made so uneasy, I ordered the tents to be struck; and, after riding five hours, we halted near a village, upon a pleasant hill about thirty miles from Larache, where we were abundantly supplied with provisions by the Cadi. From this place we had a most delightful prospect of the Atlantic Ocean to our left, and, to the right and front, an extensive forest and an immense plain of corn-fields and meadows. We set forward again at daybreak; and by pursuing our journey in the afternoon, for it was utterly impossible to travel in the middle of the day, we reached this city (Larache) late in the evening.

After breakfast next morning, as I was going up to the Castle to pay my devoirs to the worthy Governor, my attention was arrested by a great riot in the street. Perceiving four of our sailors likely to become the victims of an enraged multitude, I hastened to their relief. I found that the disturbance was occasioned by their imprudence in attempting to inspect the face of a Moorish woman. They belonged to a Gibraltar privateer, which had just arrived at this port to take in refreshment. Having drank too much *aguardiente* they imagined themselves in the streets of Gibraltar. I found no great difficulty in prevailing on the mob not to injure them, and in ensuring them a safe conduct back to their vessel. I recommended the commander of the privateer to put to sea without loss of time. The Governor not only forgave the offence, but sent plenty of fresh provisions on board for the ship's company just as the vessel was getting under way.

Commanders of armed vessels putting into a port of these states should not, on any account, suffer their men to go on shore, as they are very apt to ridicule the Moors, who are a set of people not to be trifled with. To prevent, therefore, any unpleasant occurrences, that may tend to lessen the high opinion which the Moors in general entertain of the English, and in order to defeat the views of the French party, which are incessantly directed towards forming dangerous cabals against the interest of the British nation, some effectual means ought to be applied. The Moors are very fickle, and their predilection may be converted into hatred, which is exactly the point the French aim at, to the great detriment of our fleet stationed in those seas, but particularly to the garrison of Gibraltar, and would ultimately involve us in an unprofitable war.

His Excellency has written to Lord Collingwood, to request a vessel to convey me to Gibraltar; he has very handsomely given me a copy of the letter he sent, which I inclose for your perusal.

"Larache, July 27th, 1806.

"MY LORD,

"His Imperial Majesty has been pleased to bestow on Dr. Buffa many presents, consisting of horses, mules, &c. &c. and entertains a great regard for him on account of the good he has done in Barbary; my Royal Master has also been graciously pleased to give him a letter to the King of England, intreating that the Doctor be permitted to attend the Emperor occasionally, and to reside for the future, for that service, at Tangiers or Gibraltar.

"In compliance with His Imperial Majesty's wishes, I have now most earnestly to request that your Lordship will be pleased to order Dr. Buffa a sure conveyance to the garrison of Gibraltar, and one of His Majesty's transports to receive the presents given to him, as a reward for his merit, and for his good and steady conduct during his stay with us. The Doctor carries with him the good wishes of all the Moors attached to my Royal Master; and I have the honour to assure your Lordship, that he has daily exerted himself with me, and lately with His Imperial Majesty, for the service of his

King, and for that of his fellow-subjects at Gibraltar. On this account alone I hope your Lordship will, as soon as possible, afford him an opportunity to join his family, at Gibraltar, in safety.

"I have the honour to be,

"My Lord,

"Your Lordship's

"Friend and servant,

(Signed)

"MOHAMMED ABDALLAH ESLAWEE,

Governor of Larache, &c. &c. &c.

To the Right Hon. Lord Collingwood, Admiral and Commander in Chief, &c. &c. &c.

LETTER XXIII.

Embark for Gibraltar—Precautionary Hints.

Gibraltar.

In compliance with the request of the Governor of Larache, His Majesty's hired armed ship the Lord Eldon was ordered by Lord Collingwood to convey me to this place. She arrived at Larache about a week after I wrote last. The bar unfortunately proved so bad, that she was obliged to drop her anchor on the outside; and the Captain, conceiving it an unsafe anchorage, pressed me to repair on board without delay, which I did, after taking a long farewell of my noble friend the Governor, who, with tears in his eyes, embraced me, and otherwise evinced his infinite regret and true friendship.

We embarked all my horses, mules, &c. &c. without any accident, and immediately after set sail for Tangiers. I cannot find words to describe the interesting, curious, and romantic appearance of the Barbary coast, from Larache to Tangiers, when viewed from the sea. I took my station on the quarter-deck, and, as we sailed close in shore, my curiosity was fully gratified. There are several small bays and creeks along this coast, which unfortunately afford shelter to the enemy's privateers, where, in perfect security, they remain concealed, watching an opportunity to come out and seize any of our straggling vessels that have either separated from, or are waiting for convoy to enter the Straits.

It is a great pity that the number of our gun-boats at this port (Gibraltar) is so limited, as a larger number of them, and a few other small vessels kept in readiness here, and well appointed, would protect our commerce, and prevent our suffering so much from the Spanish boats, and several small French cruizers, which infest this part of the world, and almost daily capture some of our merchant-men, which they carry into Algesiras in sight of this garrison.

APPENDIX.

No. I.

Copy of a Letter from JOHN TURNBULL, Esquire, Chairman to the Board of
Trade, to E. COOKE, Esquire, Under Secretary of State, &c. &c. &c.

SIR,

In my capacity of General Chairman of the Merchants trading to
the Mediterranean, and in consequence of the commercial relations
which I have long maintained with Gibraltar, I think it my duty to
submit, with great deference, to the consideration of Lord Castlereagh certain observations respecting the late dreadful calamity,
which afflicted that garrison. The great mortality which then prevailed, and which carried off almost the whole of the civil inhabitants,
was in a great degree to be imputed to the want of medical assistance for the poorer classes of the people, who are chiefly foreigners. The physicians and surgeons attached to the army, had every
moment of their time fully occupied by the care of the troops immediately under their charge. If even they could have spared a little
attention to the miserable objects just mentioned, it could probably
have produced but a very inadequate effect. As the medical gentle-
men could not be supposed to be acquainted with the various foreign dialects that these people could only make use of, they were
therefore obliged to be abandoned to their fate; and by their numerous deaths, and the intercourse they had with one another, neces-
sarily occasioned a deplorable increase of contagion. It is therefore
respectfully suggested, that, as the return of such a disorder ought
at any rate to be guarded against, it would be highly desirable, that
a medical gentleman, conversant with the languages of the southern

parts of Europe, should be appointed as physician to the civil inhabitants of Gibraltar, and for their express and immediate care. There is now in London, a gentleman (Doctor Buffa), Physician to His Majesty's Forces, who appears to be peculiarly well qualified for such an appointment. He is possessed of superior medical abilities, and particularly in the disorders of the plague and yellow-fever, in the treatment of which he has had much experience and success; and having been born in Piedmont, he is well acquainted with the southern languages of Europe. If Lord Castlereagh should be pleased to approve of Doctor Buffa being placed at Gibraltar, in the situation which I have taken the liberty to suggest, it would occasion no extraordinary expense to Government, Doctor Buffa being now one of the Physicians to the Army, and might eventually be productive of the most beneficial effects.

I have the honour to be, most respectfully,
SIR,
Your most obedient and
Most humble servant,
(Signed) JOHN TURNBULL.

Guilford Street, 5th August 1805.

E. Cooke, Esq. &c. &c. &c.

No. II.

Letter from the Secretary of the Transport Board to Dr. BUFFA.

Transport Office, 16th October 1805.

SIR,

I am directed by the Board to acquaint you, that a passage to Gibraltar has been provided for yourself, Mrs. Buffa, your family and brother-in-law, on board the Active transport; and that you may embark on board that ship at Deptford immediately.

I am further directed to add, that it will be necessary for you to find your own provisions.

I am, Sir,
Your most obedient servant,
A. WHITEHEAD, Secretary.

To Dr. Buffa, &c. &c. &c.

No. III.

Extract of a Letter from JOHN TURNBULL, Esq. Chairman of the Committee of Merchants trading to the Levant, &c. to Dr. BUFFA.

MY DEAR SIR,

On your arrival at Gibraltar, I was favoured with two letters from you; but have not since had the pleasure of hearing from you. Nor have I written to you, as, notwithstanding the unremitting endeavours, and the constant attention, on every occasion, of His Royal Highness and myself, it has not been in our power to do any thing effectual to serve you. The Medical Board *continue to give all the opposition that they possibly can*, and made a very unfavourable report, in consequence of a strong representation that I made in your favour to Mr. Windham.

London, 7th July 1806.

No. IV.

Extract of a Letter from JOHN ROSS, Esq. Acting Consul General at Tangiers, to Dr. BUFFA.

Friday, 7th May 1806.

DEAR SIR,

I heard only to-day of your arrival at Tetuan on your way to Larache, and this evening received an express from Indy Mahamed
Slawey, Governor of that place, to request that, if I knew you had
been in this country, you would use every possible endeavour to
come to him at Larache; and to accompany him to the Emperor who
wished to see you.

Let me therefore request your moving as quick as possible to Larache direct from Tetuan, and join him before he departs. Should
you miss him, he has left orders to his Lieutenant-governor there, to
forward you to Sidy immediately.

No. V.

Letter written to JOHN ROSS, Esq. Acting Consul General at
Tangiers.

Larache, May 17th, 1806.

SIR,

His Excellency the Governor of this place having last evening received a letter from the Emperor, inclosing a communication trans-
mitted by the French Consul, together with a note from Paris, His
Excellency has honoured me with both to peruse. Their contents
were the most severe philippics against England; our blessed
government was represented the most perfidious and treacherous
in the world, and great art used to excite distrust, and to produce a
rupture with England. M. Talleyrand informs His Imperial Majesty,
by command, of the taking of Naples, and the republic of Ragusa;
that Bonaparte, for certain political reasons, has thought it expedient to appoint Louis Bonaparte King of Holland; and Joseph, his
other brother, King of the Two Sicilies: that it was Bonaparte's de-

termination to exclude the English from every port in Europe: that Ceuta should, as soon as an opportunity offers, be occupied entirely by French troops; that Spain and Portugal would soon become provinces of France, and that His Imperial Majesty could do no better thing than to abandon the English, and make common cause with France: that the French Consul was charged to demand five thousand bullocks, as many horses and mules; wheat and barley for the French forces: that an equivalent in territory should be given to the Emperor, and a certain scheme submitted to the Court of Morocco highly honourable and advantageous to Barbary.

I told His Excellency to be on his guard; for that, by art, Bonaparte has enslaved, plundered, and overturned the continent of Europe: that I could not help ridiculing the idea of exporting provisions and cattle from Barbary: that Bonaparte might cause them to be exported by air-balloons, but by no other means or conveyance, while England rules the seas. I availed myself of this opportunity of delineating the features of the Great Nation, and relating the acts and deeds of Bonaparte at Alexandria, Acre, and Jaffa; which had the desired effect. He then confidentially informed me, that the Emperor had commanded him to reply to the French government as he deemed most conducive to the interest and good of Barbary: that he should cut matters short: that proper steps should be taken to defeat their cabals and intrigues, and a watchful eye kept for the future on the motions of the French Consul, and all his agents; and that I might assure the British government, that his influence shall always be used for the interests of the English. Upon which I thanked him, and told him that the Emperor might always command my services, whenever he deemed them necessary.

You will no longer apprehend the ascendancy of the French in this part of the world, as it is all over with them; nor will they ever succeed as long as this excellent Moorish Chief guides the councils of thee Emperor.

I remain, with due respect,

SIR,

Your Most obedient servant,

JOHN BUFFA.

To John Ross, Esq.
Acting Consul General, '
Tangiers.

No. VI.

Letter from Captain STEWART, of His Majesty's
Ship Seahorse, to — —.

His Britannic Majesty's Frigate Seahorse, June 1806.

MOST NOBLE AND EXCELLENT SIR,

Presuming on the great friendship between our royal masters, I have sent an officer on shore to request of you, leave to purchase some cattle, sheep, and fowls, for myself, my officers and crew, who have been long cruizing without fresh provisions. He is authorized to draw bills on the British government for the amount of the purchase, which I will approve and sign.

The quantity of cattle we want, will be about twenty-five, of sheep about eighteen, and of fowls about twelve dozen (besides some eggs and vegetables), more or less, according to the price.

May the light of Heaven be shed upon you many years!

I have the honour to be, with great respect,
Your most obedient humble servant,
JOHN STEWART, Captain.

No. VII.

Letter from Lord COLLINGWOOD to His
Excellency the Governor of Larache.

Ocean, off Cadiz, 8th July 1806.

MOST EXCELLENT GOVERNOR,

I have received the letter which Your Excellency directed to be wrote by Dr. Buffa to one of my officers who sent to Larache for stock; and I beg to express to you the great satisfaction I have in every instance which demonstrates the friendship which is entertained, by His Imperial Majesty, for the King of Great Britain, and his subjects; and to assure Your Excellency, that, on my part, I shall always be happy in every opportunity of shewing you, that the same sentiment of friendship and kindness is felt by us towards the Moors.

I am much obliged to Your Excellency for the supplies of refreshment, which you are pleased to offer to my ships, which may call at Larache. And wishing you health,

I am,

Most excellent Governor,

Your friend and servant.

COLLINGWOOD.

To His Excellency

the Governor of Larache.

No. VIII.

Letter to the Right Honourable Lord COLLINGWOOD, &c. &c. &c.

Michanez, July 16th, 1808.

MY LORD,

I am instructed by His Excellency the Governor of Larache, and principal minister of the Emperor of Morocco, to acknowledge the receipt of your Lordship's letter, directed to him at Larache, of the 8th instant, and feel great satisfaction in being able thus to convey

His Excellency's assurance to your Lordship, that nothing shall be wanting on his part to forward (which is verbatim what he directed me to write) the interest of the English, as long as he shall retain any influence with his royal master; that he has always felt great pleasure in promoting the views and wishes of the late English Consul, and shall ever continue the same.

He has represented to His Imperial Majesty the affair of the French privateer, which was driven on shore near Tangiers, by one of your Lordship's small vessels. His Excellency commands me to inform your Lordship, that His Imperial Majesty highly approves of the noble and generous conduct of the English on that occasion, and deprecates that of the French, lamenting, that when the marauders landed on the Moorish shore, his subjects did not put every Frenchman to death.

His Imperial Majesty greatly laments the undeserved treatment which was offered near Tetuan to one of your Lordship's officers, by an unworthy officer under the command of Governor Ash-Ash. His Imperial Majesty, at His Excellency's representation, solicited by me, has written, some time since, a letter to Ash-Ash, strictly enjoining and commanding him to favour the interest of the English only, and not to take any French part directly or indirectly, on pain of His Majesty's eternal displeasure; the more so, as His Imperial Majesty's solicitude and resolve is now to keep up that friendship and good understanding which has hitherto been evinced on all occasions on the part of the King of Britain, and His Imperial Majesty, who desires to be made known to your Lordship his decided partiality to the English. His Excellency wishes your Lordship health and prosperity.

I have the honour to be, my Lord,

Your Lordship's

Most obedient humble servant,

J. BUFFA.

To His Excellency
Lord Collingwood,

&c. &c. &c.

By order of Mahomed Abdalah Eslawee,
Governor of Larache, and first Minister
to the Emperor.

No. IX.

Translation of a Letter written by His Excellency the Governor of
Larache, And first Minister to the Emperor of Morocco, to the Right
Honourable Lord COLLINGWOOD.

Larache, July 27th, 1806.

His Imperial Majesty having been pleased to permit Doctor Buffa
to return to Gibraltar, and entertaining a great regard for him, on
account of the good he has done in Barbary, the Emperor has also
been pleased to testify the same in a letter written with his own
hand, to the King of Great Britain, strongly pressing His Majesty
that the Doctor may be permitted to attend him occasionally, and to
reside upon a fixed appointment at Gibraltar. In compliance with
His Imperial Majesty's wishes, I have now most earnestly to request
that your Lordship will be pleased to order him a sure and commodious conveyance for Gibraltar, and to take in the presents he has
received as a reward for his merit, and for his good and steady
conduct during his stay with us. The Doctor carries with him the
good wishes of all the Moors attached to my Royal and Imperial
Master; and I have the honour to assure your Lordship, that he has
daily exerted himself with me, and lately with the Emperor, for the
service of His Majesty's navy, and for the garrison of Gibraltar.

On this account alone, I hope your Lordship will, as soon as possible, afford him an opportunity of joining his family in safety.

Health and prosperity.

(Signed)
MAHOMED BEN ABDALAH ESLAWEE.

No. X.

Translation of a Letter, in the Arabic Language, from Sultan
SOLYMAN BEN MAHOMED, Emperor of Morocco, to His Majesty
GEORGE the Third, King of Great Britain, &c, &c, &c. &c.

In the name of God, the all-merciful and commiserating God; on
whom is our account, and whose support we acknowledge; for
there is neither creation, nor power, but that which proceeds from
God, the high and eternal God.

From the servant of God, the commander of the faithful in
Mahomed, upheld and supported by the grace of God, Solyman the
son of Mahomed, the son of Abd' Allah, the son of Ismael, Prince of
Hassenie, ever upheld by the power of God, Sultan of Fez, of
Morocco, of Suze, of Dea'ha, of Tafilet, and of Tuat, together with all
the territories of the Garban West.

```
    / — — — — — — —\
   / L .S. \
   / Solyman the \
   | Son of Mahommed, |
   | &c. &c. |
   | God illumine |
   | and support |
   \ him, /
    \ &c. &c. /
     \— — — — — — —/
```

To our cherished, our dearly beloved brother (who is exalted by
the power of God), Sultan George the Third, Sultan of the territories
of the United Kingdom of Great Britain and Ireland, Duke of Meck-
lenberg, Prince descended from the line or dynasty of the Emperors
of Rome and Palestine.

This premised, we inform you, that we continually make diligent and friendly inquiry concerning you, desiring from our heart, that you may be at all times surrounded by wealth and prosperity. We wish you to increase in friendship with us, that our alliance may be stronger than heretofore, even stronger than it was in the days of our ancestors, whom God guard and protect. Now therefore we make known to you, that your physician and servant Dr. Buffa has been in our royal presence, which is exalted by the bounty of God; and we have been pleased with his medical knowledge and diligent attention; and moreover with the relief he hath given to us. We have therefore to entreat or to ask of you, to give him your royal order to return to our neighbourhood, to Gibraltar, well provided with all good and necessary medicines; that he, residing at Gibraltar, may be ready to attend quickly on our royal person, whenever we may stand in need of his medical assistance: we trust you will therefore return him immediately without delay or procrastination; seeing that he has been of essential service to us. And we recommend you to exalt Dr. Buffa in your favour, and we will always be your allies and friends. May you be ever surrounded by wealth and prosperity! Peace be with you! The fourth day of the month of Jumad Elute, in the year of the Hágira 1222, answering to the fifth or sixth of July 1807.

Done into the English as literally as the incompatibility of the idioms of the two languages would admit of, by JAMES GRAY JACKSON, professor of African and Arabic languages.

Fenchurch Buildings, July 1807.

No. XI.

Translations from the Arabic. The first received the 18th January; the latter, 6th July, 1808.

In the name of God, from Mahomed Ben Abdalah Eslawee, Governor of Tetuan, Tangiers, and its dependencies, &c. &c. &c.

To Doctor BUFFA.

Since your departure from us, we have not received any letter, nor heard from you; so not having heard any thing of you, we are much uneasy and concerned about you: for we love you. We are ordered by the sacred commands of our Sultan, to require you will acquaint us how you are, if any thing has happened you; and that you will return to us with an answer to the sacred letter entrusted to you, with a fresh supply of medicines, according to your promise.

We also request you will endeavour to obtain from the English Government, two masts for a frigate, of forty-five feet each, which you will cause to be sent by a frigate to Larache; and all the expense which may occur, will be paid without fail. We hope you will assist as much as possible in this business; and we wish you health, prosperity, and a speedy return among us.

(Signed)

MAHOMED BEN ABDALAH ESLAWEE.

In the Year of the Hágira 1223.

No. XII.

The second Letter, prefaced as the former, to Doctor BUFFA.

We have continued to make incessant inquiries after you, but all to no purpose. What has become, or befallen you, we know not; nothing, we hope, very bad. We consider you a very good man, honest and honourable; you cannot wilfully forfeit your sacred pledge, your promise, your honour to return to us. We were afraid you were dead, but we heard lately you are alive, and resident in London. Return then to the presence of our great Sultan, and every thing you will reasonably ask for your nation shall be granted to your nation, shall be granted to you. The supplies shall be increased to Gibraltar, and you will be treated as before, and, if possible, better still; for we love you. Return then without fear to the presence of our great Sultan, and prove yourself a true Englishman, by keeping your promise. We wish you good health and prosperity.

(Signed)

MAHOMED BEN ABDALAH ESLAWEE.

Tetuan.

In the Year of the Hágira 1223.